THE BEST IN TENT CAMPING:

NORTHERN CALIFORNIA

A Guide for Campers Who Hate RVs, Concrete Slabs, and Loud Portable Stereos

Second Edition

THE BEST IN TENT CAMPING:

NORTHERN CALIFORNIA

*A Guide for Campers Who Hate RVs, Concrete Slabs,
and Loud Portable Stereos*

Second Edition

Bill Mai

Menasha
Ridge
Press, Inc.

Library of Congress Cataloging-in-Publication Data

Mai, Bill, 1945–
    The best in tent camping, northern California : a guide for campers who hate
RVs, concrete slabs, and loud portable stereos / Bill Mai.—2nd ed.
        p. cm.
    Includes bibliographical references (p. 165).
    ISBN 0-89732-399-8
    1. Camp sites, facilities, etc.—California, Northern—Guidebooks.
2. Camping—California, Northern—Guidebooks.   3. California,
Northern—Guidebooks.   I. Title.
    GV191.42.C2 M246 2001
                                                                2001034266
                                                                CIP

Cover design by Grant Tatum
Cover photo by Dennis Coello
Maps by Brian Taylor

Menasha Ridge Press
P.O. Box 43673
Birmingham, Alabama 35243
www.menasharidge.com

Best in Tent Camping

CONTENTS

The Cascade Range

The Sierra Nevada

MAP LEGEND

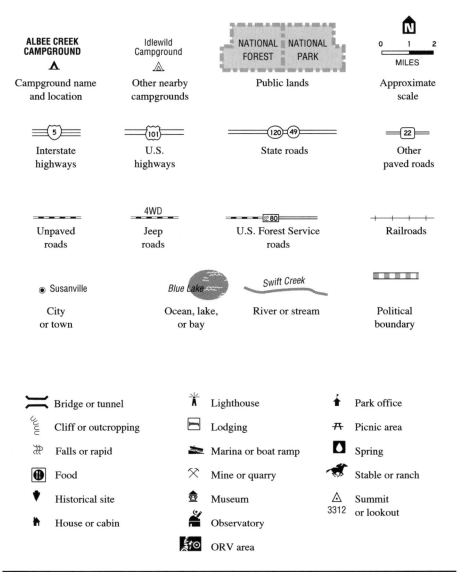

ALBEE CREEK CAMPGROUND ▲	Idlewild Campground ◬	NATIONAL FOREST NATIONAL PARK	N 0 1 2 MILES
Campground name and location	Other nearby campgrounds	Public lands	Approximate scale

5	101	120 49	22
Interstate highways	U.S. highways	State roads	Other paved roads

Unpaved roads	4WD Jeep roads	80 U.S. Forest Service roads	Railroads

⊙ Susanville	*Blue Lake*	*Swift Creek*	
City or town	Ocean, lake, or bay	River or stream	Political boundary

Bridge or tunnel	Lighthouse	Park office
Cliff or outcropping	Lodging	Picnic area
Falls or rapid	Marina or boat ramp	Spring
Food	Mine or quarry	Stable or ranch
Historical site	Museum	Summit or lookout 3312
House or cabin	Observatory	
	ORV area	

CAMPGROUNDS

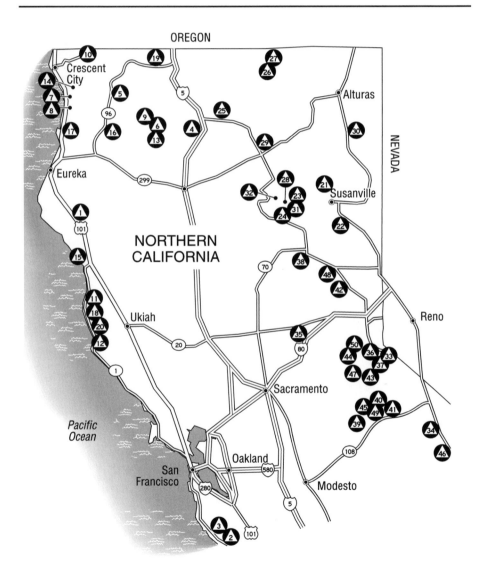

PREFACE

Friends and family get together, and pretty soon somebody starts talking about going camping, fishing the streams, and hiking the high country, and suddenly everybody wants to go. Usually the proposed trip fizzles out the next morning because nobody knows quite where to go or how to arrange it, and nobody wants to end up camping in a little tent on a slab of concrete surrounded by hard-partying RVers. Nobody knows a sure-good campground, so the whole camping adventure dies on the vine.

Well, that's why you buy this book. You'll discover 50 of the most wonderful spots to tent camp in Northern California and learn how to reserve a spot if necessary, what to expect, and how to get there. All 50 campgrounds will be clean, safe, well run, and beautiful in their own way.

The 50 best are along the coast or in the mountains. Each of the campgrounds is rated in categories of beauty, site privacy, site spaciousness, quiet, security, and cleanliness/upkeep, so you pick the best from the best. There's not a loser here. Your choice will depend on what you like and what time of year you want to go camping.

I selected my 50 best by going camping, by finding the tent-friendly campgrounds, by talking to rangers, and by buttonholing other campers or locals and asking them their favorite spot. I tried to be objective. I reined in my preference for big country pine and boulder-style campgrounds and gave the nod to some campgrounds located deep in the woods. I spaced out the campgrounds; I picked geographically as well as seasonally; and I stayed away from very small campgrounds because even if a few folks show up, they're full.

When you get out and start camping, you'll find your own hit parade of campgrounds. You'll stumble upon all the tiny gems with three or four sites and explore all the fantastic places in the mountains and along the coast where you can camp anywhere you want. It's a whole new world.

—*Bill Mai*

THE BEST IN TENT CAMPING:

NORTHERN CALIFORNIA

A Guide for Campers Who Hate RVs, Concrete Slabs, and Loud Portable Stereos

Second Edition

INTRODUCTION

A Word about This Book and Northern California Camping

Camp Northern California. Drive up I-5 and feel the big granite block of the Sierra Nevada looming to the east, 400 miles long. Ahead is Mount Shasta, 14,161 feet high and topped with snow. To the west is the Coast Range, an ocean of sharp mountains and redwoods dipping down into the Pacific itself, where the white blue of waves break on rocky shore. From Lassen Volcanic National Park north, the Cascade Range is all volcanic, up past Alturas to Lava Beds National Monument and the borders. The weather is as wild as the land. Nowhere else can you feel so remote, camp on such wild, beautiful land, and fish the last untamed river running to the sea.

Geography

For the purposes of this book, Northern California is everything above a line drawn from Santa Cruz across the top of Yosemite National Park to the Nevada border. This area is divided into the Coast Range, the Cascade Range, and the Sierra Nevada.

The Coast Range includes the hundreds of miles of rock cliffs, sandy coves, and beaches between Santa Cruz and Oregon, as well as the mountains running down to the sea—the King Range, the Siskiyous, the Marble Mountains, the Trinity Alps—and the rivers—the untamed Smith, the Klamath, and the Salmon. East of I-5 is the Cascade Range in the north, the Modoc plateau, and Mount Shasta and Lassen Volcanic National Park, where the Cascade Range flows south and merges with the Sierra Nevada. Here, in the Sierra Nevada, good summer weather offers the best mountain camping in California.

Where to go and when

September and October are best, but camp the coast all year long. Watch the weather. Big storms in the winter blow in and wash out roads. There can be months of fog. In the winter the wind can blow like hell. Then, suddenly the sky will be warm and sunny and clear. The coastal clime is an inconsistent tyrant: very bad when bad, and sweet as pie when good. Fog can be fun. Rain can be fun. And they sure make you appreciate the sun.

Camping the mountains is mostly for late spring, summer, and early fall. The Sierra Nevada climate is fairly reliable as soon as the winter snow pack melts. Farther north, watch the weather. It can get bone cold even in the summer.

Some mountain campgrounds in Northern California are open even in the winter for the hardy breed who want to snow camp. Watch the weather and come prepared. For dead-cert warm-winter camping, forget Northern California and head south to Death Valley, Anza Borrego, or Baja California.

The rating system

The 50 best campgrounds are rated in various categories—five stars is best, and one star is acceptable. Use the rating system to select the wonderful campground that combines the elements that best suit you.

Beauty

Although all 50 campgrounds in this book are beautiful, some are absolutely sensational. They rate five stars. Mountains, streams, waterfalls, and sunsets all conspire for a drop-dead campground personality. One- to four-star campgrounds are no dogs, either, but possess a less spectacular beauty that will grow on you.

Site privacy

Some campgrounds are beautifully built. The sites are arranged to take maximum advantage of the contour of the land, and the vegetation gives each one the most privacy possible. Good architecture cuts down on the cringe factor when other campers pull in next door. It makes you feel at home from the moment you step out of your car. What a difference!

Site spaciousness

I want flat land to pitch a tent on. And, I want the flat area far enough from the picnic table so my camping mate can make coffee without waking me, and far enough away from the firepit so the embers don't burn little holes in the tent. And, I want a view. A view from each campsite is part of the spacious feeling that qualifies a campground for five stars in this category.

Quiet

Quiet is part of beautiful. There's nothing like the sound of a generator or a boom box to ruin a beautiful campsite. I consider white noise like the roar of a river to raise the quiet rating, since it is a natural noise and drowns out the sounds of other campers.

Security

Most of the campsites in the top 50 have campground hosts that keep a good eye on the property, which makes the campground safer than a good neighborhood. The farther the campground is from an urban center, the more secure it is. Of course, you can leave your valuables with the hosts if you're going to be gone for a day or so, but don't leave little things lying around. A blue jay will take off with a pair of sunglasses, and you never can tell what a visiting bear will decide has food value.

Cleanliness/upkeep

Most campgrounds in the top 50 are well tended. Sometimes, on big weekends, places can get a little rank—not unlike one's kitchen after a big party. I appreciate the little things, like the campground host who came around with a rake after each site was vacated to police the place. That particular campground received five stars in the cleanliness/upkeep department.

Good planning

A little planning makes a good camping trip great. First, decide where and when you want to go. Then, phone that district's Ranger H.Q. to make sure the campground is open and that it has water. See if the ranger recommends other campgrounds. See if it's going to be busy. If it is, reserve ahead if possible. All national forest campgrounds must be reserved at least ten days in advance. Remember, if you arrive and don't like the reserved site, the campground host will move you if another site is available.

Next, get your equipment together. Everybody knows what basics to bring tent camping. A tent (of course), the sleeping bags, a cooler, a stove, pots, utensils, a water jug, matches, a can opener, and so forth. But, it's those little things that you suddenly wish you had that make a happy camper. Number one objective is a good night's sleep.

Bring earplugs. You need ear plugs to get a good snooze. The first night or two out camping, the unfamiliar flap of the tent drives you crazy if you don't have earplugs. Also, a snoring mate sleeping a foot away from you is nighttime hell on earth without earplugs. In addition, earplugs block out all that night nature stuff that interferes with a righteous camper's zzzzzs.

Don't forget to pack your own pillow. A good pillow gets your shoulders off the deck and lets your hips and behind take the weight. Use your clothes bag as an additional pillow (consider inflatable pillows sold at camping stores). Bring a thin foam mattress or buy the self-inflating pads (phone Basic Design at (320) 252-1642). Buy a Spidermat—a device that keeps your pad from slipping on the tent floor and keeps your sleeping bag on top of it. Air mattresses are okay but susceptible to puncture. Never buy a double air mattress—every time your mate moves you get tossed around. Get a sleeping bag that is good and warm. Nothing is worse than being cold at night, and no sleeping bag is too warm. Just bring a sheet so you can sleep under it at first, then crawl into the bag when it gets nippy. Check the weather. If it's going to be cold, remember to bring socks and sweatpants to sleep in. A sweatshirt with a hood is invaluable, since you lose a lot of heat through your head.

Bring a water bottle to drink from at night. Consequently, a pee jar (a pee pot for ladies) just outside the tent is a great idea. You can stumble outside, use it, and empty it in the toilet in the morning.

Nothing disturbs your zzzzs like grit inside the tent, so bring something to put outside the tent to clean your feet on. In the woods, a square of AstroTurf works fine. At the seashore or in the desert, a tray full of water to dip your feet in works best. Bring a small brush for what grit leaks in.

Remember flashlights. The little mini-mags work okay, and if you take off the lens, you can hang them from a tent loop and actually read. Be careful since the little bulb is damn hot and will burn fabric or fingers. But, what works even better is a head lamp. You can buy them at any outdoor store. Just strap the lamp around your head with an adjustable elastic band. Everywhere you look, there's light. They're great for finding stuff, cleaning up in the dark after dinner, and reading. Remember duct tape. "If you can't fix it, duct tape it" is a camping maxim.

Bring a sponge to clean off the picnic table. A plastic tablecloth is nice, too (bring little pushpins to secure it so it won't blow away). A plastic bowl or a blow-up sink from Basic Designs (around $6 at Sportmart) is invaluable for washing dishes. Picnic table benches get mighty hard, so bring a cushion. Buy a cheap lawn chair, and get the inexpensive umbrella that attaches to the back of the chair, so you can sit around camp out of the sun. While sitting around, you'll want a fly swatter to wreak revenge on a lazy droning fly or two and mosquito repellent for that irksome gnat in your ear. Bring a little leaf rake to police your camp area. Remember binoculars, a bird book, and a wildflower book, so you can put a name with what you see.

Good water jugs are two-and-a-half-gallon plastic jobs sold in supermarkets. On most of them, you can twist the top off and refill them. They travel best with their valves up to avoid any leakage. Take a hot shower. Basic Designs (and other outfits) sells a solar shower bag that really works. After a day in the sun sitting on a hot rock, the water is hot! Or, bring along nonscented diaper wipes for a quick sponge bath. They work.

Don't be afraid to ask fellow campers for help or for stuff you might have forgotten. All campers know what it's like to forget basic stuff and love to help fellow campers. There's always a mechanic on vacation camping at the next site over when your car won't start, or somebody with extra white gas for your stove. Think hearty about your fellow campers. Wave and say, "Hi."

The campfire is an important camp event. Stores around the campground sell bundles of wood, and often, the campground host and hostess sell wood. Also, there may be windfalls around the campground from which you can take wood (ask the campground host). You need a good camp saw for that. An absolute essential is a can of charcoal starter fluid. This guarantees a fire even in a driving rain. Naturally, don't forget marshmallows, graham crackers, and chocolate for roasting.

Fix your car up before you go. Nothing can be a bigger bummer than a mechanical breakdown on your way. Have a mechanic check your water hoses and the air pressure in your tires before you load up. Remember, your car will be loaded down with stuff, and this will put a strain on your tires and cooling system. Bring an extra fan belt. Nothing can shut down the car like a snapped fan belt that you have to special order from Japan. Even if you don't know a fan belt from third base, bring one. Somebody will come along who knows how to install it. Make sure your spare tire is correctly inflated. Mishap #999 is when you put on your spare, let the car down, and find out the spare is flat.

If you fish, be sure to get a license and display it. Fishing without a license is a misdemeanor, punishable by a maximum fine of $1,000 and/or six months in jail. On your way into the campground, stop at a local store and find out what the folks are using for bait. Buy it. This will save you a lot of experimentation and probably provide you with a good meal.

Remember the bears. Never leave your cooler out. Put it in the trunk or disguise it with a blanket if you have a hatchback or a van. Don't eat in your tent. Take all cosmetics, soap, etc. and put them in the car. Disguise them, too. A bear will rip off a car door to get a tube of Chap Stick. Bring a small bottle of Clorox to wipe down the picnic table at night. Bears don't like Clorox (but don't put too much faith in this!). If a bear raids your camp looking for food, beat on pots and pans and shoo him away like you would a naughty dog. Don't worry. Even the boldest of bears won't even dream of going into a tent unless it smells food.

Don't forget about mosquitoes. Where you have rain, trees, and rivers, there's mosquitoes—and they're hungry. Bring a couple different kinds of repellent since there are 3,000 kinds of mosquitoes. Repellent some mosquitoes detest others find very attractive. I like 3M's Ultrathon repellent—this is serious stuff. And, sometimes, Avon's Skin-So-Soft works wonders. Other times, it draws mosquitoes from miles away. A great idea if you are going to camp for a couple days is a screen house. You can set it up over the picnic table or in a sunny spot and lounge in there while less-prepared neighbors are under siege. Coleman sells one for just over $100 for light duty—Eureka sells a sturdier, larger one for, of course, many more bucks.

Think about swimming. Bring old tennis shoes or buy water booties for wading in streams and in lakes. Goggles are cool to check out what the trout are doing. Bring any rubber flotation device you can afford and carry in your auto that will get your highly vulnerable body on the gorgeous blue mountain lakes but definitely out of the frigid water. Think Big 5's Sevylor $50 blowups with an air pump driven off the cigarette lighter of the car. They are lightweight and fun, but never set your device down on sharp shale or pine needles—and come prepared with a repair kit.

Think about dispersed camping. With a fire permit, a shovel, and a bucket of water, you can camp just about anywhere in the national forests (consult the Ranger District H.Q.). The fire permit costs nothing, and there are miles and miles of fire roads and lumber roads you can explore to find the dispersed campground of your dreams.

Settling in

When you come into a campground, be aware of a certain psychological barrier. This is a new place. Suddenly, you've driven all this way, and the campground doesn't look that hot. You feel disappointed. You feel like the "new kid at school." The other campers look up from their game of gin rummy and hope you won't camp next to them as you drive around the campground loops and look helplessly at the open sites. Nothing looks good enough.

Park your car. Pull into the first available site that could possibly do. Then, walk around the campground. You have half an hour to decide before you pick your site and pay. Once you get out and walk, you'll break through that "new kid at school" dilemma and soon feel like you're a part of the place. It's odd. Suddenly, you don't mind camping next to the gin rummy players. You realize that this is your campground as well as theirs. By the next morning, the whole place will feel like home, and the gin rummy players will seem like the best of neighbors. You won't understand why you didn't immediately recognize this campground as the best of all campgrounds.

When you plan a camping trip, try to stay in one campground for at least three days. Stay one day, and you end up spending most of your time packing and unpacking and getting familiar with the campground. Stay three days and you'll relax and have fun.

Go tent camping. Live in paradise for a few days. Camping makes you want to sin like the damned, sleep like the righteous, and hike like the last of the great American walkers. Balm for the weary soul!

NORTHERN CALIFORNIA

THE COAST

THE COAST

ALBEE CREEK CAMPGROUND

Humboldt Redwoods State Park, near Garberville

D rive 5 miles off Highway 101 on Mattole Road through incredible stands of Redwoods (use daytime headlights), and come to Albee Creek Campground 0.3 mile up an access road on the right. This beautiful campground is framed by Albee Creek on the east and Bull Creek to the south—most of the campsites nestle into the north at the base of a forested hillside. This is nice open camping for folks who don't want the "darkness at noon" aspect of the redwood forest. Down below on the little prairie is an old fruit orchard planted by John Albee, who carried mail into Bull Valley in the old days before the forest became Humboldt Redwoods State Park.

From Albee Campground catch the Big Trees–Albee Creek Loop Trail. This is a 2.5-mile round-trip hike that follows Albee Creek east as it meanders just south of Mattole Road through the Rockefeller Forest, the world's largest grove of old-growth redwood. The average age of these trees falls between 500 and 1,200 years, with the oldest-known tree at 2,200 years old. Many measure over 300 feet high, with some topping 360 feet. Hike under these trees among the calypso orchids, fetid adder's tongues, and redwood sorrel, and think about what the trees meant to the Native Americans in this region. They used them to make dugout canoes, plank and bark houses, and furniture. The shredded inner bark made women's skirts.

CAMPGROUND RATINGS

Beauty:	★★★★★
Site privacy:	★★★
Site spaciousness:	★★★★
Quiet:	★★★
Security:	★★★★★
Cleanliness/upkeep:	★★★★

Come out of the Big Trees into the sunshine. Albee Campground is a pretty little spot.

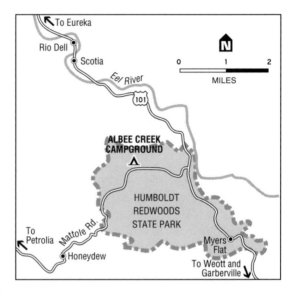

The first strangers to see the redwoods were the Chinese more than 2,000 years ago. Accounts tell of a junk captain, Hee-li, who followed his compass in the direction he thought was east (what did he think when he saw the sun setting in the east instead of the west?). Four months later he landed in a place with wonderful weather and gigantic trees with thick, reddish bark. Hee-li checked out his compass and found a small cockroach wedged under the needle. Upon his removal of the cockroach, the needle swung around, and Hee-li sailed back home to China.

Next came the Spanish missionaries, who saw the redwoods near Monterey and cut them for roof beams in the missions. They soon realized the *palo colorado* had wonderful properties. Father Junipero Serra had his coffin made of redwood. A century later his exhumed coffin was in perfect condition.

Then Dr. Josiah Gregg and a group of forty-niners came through these parts and discovered Humboldt Bay (which he named after his hero, Alexander von Humboldt, the 19th-century German scientist, naturalist, and geographer). Then gold was discovered on the Trinity and the Klamath. Forty-niners flooded north in 1850, and Humboldt County, with its wonderful bay and bountiful redwoods, was on its way to being the most populated region on the northern coast.

A big draw in the park is the Eel River, with springtime canoeing and the wildflower bloom. Hike down along the Eel. Pick up the River Trail where the Big Trees–Albee Creek Trail loops back around near the Rockefeller Loop. From here, the River Trail heads down the west side of the Eel to the Children's

Forest, where a stone marker records the names of local children who died in the early 1900s. The fire-hollowed trees here once were goose pens. Round-trip just tops 5 miles.

As tame as Albee Creek, Bull Creek, and the Eel River look in the summer and fall, think twice. In 1955 and 1964 there were monster floods. On the way from Garberville on Highway 101, look for the markers far above the highway that record the level of the raging water at the height of the flood. In 1955, near Albee Campground, Bull Creek raged through the town of Bull Creek, taking out 35 houses and the cemetery. Later, coffins were found in the branches of redwoods in the Rockefeller Forest.

Drive west on Mattole Road to Panther Gap (Elevation: 2,477 feet), and look over the watershed that these creeks and river service. When excessive logging cleared away the trees, there was nothing to stop the rain running off the slopes. The locals are thus caught on the horns of a dilemma. Many work for the lumber companies, but none of them want to see their houses swept away when the floods come.

Continue over Panther Gap down to the picturesque little hamlet of Honeydew (named for the sweet-tasting aphid dew beneath cottonwoods down by the river). There's good fishing on the Mattole River between Honeydew and Petrolia, home of the Hideaway Bar and Grill near the Lindley Bridge. They have delicious cinnamon rolls and hamburgers.

Humboldt Redwoods State Park has huge trees and huge mosquitoes in the late spring and summer. Prepare!

> To get there: from Weott north of Garberville, drive 2 miles north to Mattole Road, and drive west 5 miles to Albee Creek Campground entrance on the right. Go 0.3 mile up the access road to the campground.

KEY INFORMATION

Albee Creek Campground
Humboldt Redwoods
State Park
P.O. Box 100
Weott, CA 95571

Operated by: California Department of Parks and Recreation

Information: (707) 946-2409; http://parks.ca.gov; www.humboldtredwoods.org

Open: May through September

Individual sites: 14 sites for tents, 20 sites for RVs

Each site has: Picnic table, fireplace, food locker

Registration: At entrance; reserve by phone, (800) 444-7275, or online, www.reserveamerica.com

Facilities: Water, flush toilets, coin-operated showers (25¢), wood for sale

Parking: At individual site

Fee: $12 per night; $8.65 nonrefundable reservation fee

Elevation: 320 feet

Restrictions:

Pets—On leash only

Fires—In fireplace only

Vehicles—RVs up to 33 feet

Other— 15-day stay limit in the summer; reservations strongly recommended on holiday and summer weekends

BIG BASIN REDWOODS STATE PARK
near Santa Cruz

This park is the granddaddy of all the incredible California state parks. Big Basin has wonderful camping as well as tent cabins with interior wood stoves. Lovely Wastahi Campground is all walk-in tent campsites, with the farthest campsite 200 feet from the parking areas. Huckleberry is all walk-in as well, with the farthest site 50 feet from the parking. With Blooms Campground and Sempervirens Campground, Big Basin has another 102 developed campsites for RVs, but the park doesn't feel at all crowded. The huge redwoods give Big Basin a certain eerie calm.

On May 15, 1900, Andrew P. Hill camped at the base of Slippery Rock with 50 other conservationists. Together they formed the Sempervirens Club. Named for the *Sequoia sempervirens,* or redwood, the club was able to fend off the lumbermen and promote the creation of California's first state park from a deed of 3,800 acres of primeval forest. Now Big Basin has 16,000 ocean-facing acres of Santa Cruz Mountain full of redwoods, Doug fir, knob-cone pine, oak, marsh, and chaparral, thanks to the Save the Redwoods League and the Sempervirens Fund.

To get to know Big Basin, you have to hike or mountain bike. Driving an automobile in these mountain areas is chiefly a white-knuckle blur of naked fear, brake lights, and squealing tires. Pull over, park the car, and put on your hiking boots.

CAMPGROUND RATINGS

Beauty:	★★★★★
Site privacy:	★★★★
Site spaciousness:	★★★★
Quiet:	★★★
Security:	★★★★★
Cleanliness/upkeep:	★★★★

Big Basin Redwoods State Park has it all—good tent camping, tent cabins, great hiking, the marbled murrelet, and it is near Santa Cruz.

First, take the little Red-wood Nature Trail loop to pay respects to an ancient redwood grove on the flat above Opal Creek. Look for azaleas blooming in early summer and pick huckleberries in August. You'll see Big Basin's tallest tree, the 329-feet Mother of the Forest, the big-girthed Father of the Forest, and the Chimney Tree. Mother's roots pull 500 gallons of water up from the ground, which she releases as moisture into the air—no wonder the forest is dank and lush.

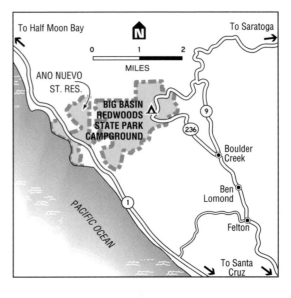

Another quick hike is up the Sequoia Trail to Sempervirens Falls. The trailhead is right by Park Headquarters, and the trail is signed for Sempervirens Falls on the way up and Park Headquarters on the way back. The forest floor is bedded with ferns, and in the spring you'll see trillium, wild ginger, and azaleas blooming. Sempervirens Falls cascades by fallen redwoods into a crystal-clear pool. Round-trip the hike is about 4 miles, although you can cut a mile or two off if you pick up the trail from Wastahi or Huckleberry Campgrounds.

The 12-mile hike everybody comes to Big Basin for is down to Berry Creek Falls. You start out at Park Headquarters and hike through the redwoods, up over the ridge, and down 4 miles to magnificent Berry Creek Falls, with a 70-foot drop to a clear pool and more cascades, fringed with ferns. I saw these falls first after a rainstorm in the sudden light of the sun—so beautiful, I thought, Great Spirit, why are you speaking to unworthy me with my day pack full of bologna sandwiches and a plastic baggie of dill pickles?

To get back, hike on up the staircase past Cascade Falls, Silver Falls, and Golden Falls, and follow Sunset Trail back to Park Headquarters.

Big Basin is home to black-tailed deer, raccoons, skunks, and squirrels. Rangers put up notices about mountain lions, but nobody ever sees the big cats. Even the Native Americans called them "ghosts." As rare as mountain lions are marbled murrelets. These robin-sized seabirds hunt fish in the ocean. Nobody had ever seen them nest until, in 1974, somebody discovered a murrelet nest made of live moss up in a Big Basin redwood. In bird-watching circles, a murrelet sighting is a great coup.

The nearest supplies are in Boulder Creek, but you want to go down to Santa Cruz and at least hike along the old half-mile boardwalk. Kids will want to ride the chilling Typhoon, the horrific Hurricane, or the terror-inspiring Wave Jammer. Adults may prefer the Giant Dipper roller coaster (circa 1924) that comes from a more genteel era. There are serious beaches here in Santa Cruz, great bookstores, a major university (even if the school mascot is the banana slug), two brew pubs, and some good places to chow down—like Aldo's at the west end of the yacht harbor.

Before you leave Big Basin, check out the 35 tent cabins on a loop road at Huckleberry Camp. Each has two full-sized beds and a wood stove, and they rent for $38 per night. Next time you need a weekend off and don't want to mount a camping trip, these babies are the answer. Bring your own sleeping bags and pillows and wood for the stove if the season's chilly.

To get there: from Santa Cruz, go north on Highway 9 for 12 miles to Boulder Creek. Turn left on Highway 236, and drive 9 miles to the Big Basin Redwoods State Park entrance.

KEY INFORMATION

Big Basin Redwoods State Park
21600 Big Basin Highway
Boulder Creek, CA 95006-9064

Operated by: California Department of Parks and Recreation

Information: (831) 338-8860; http://parks.ca.gov

Open: All year

Individual sites: 102 drive-to sites for tents or RVs, 45 easy walk-to tent sites, 4 or 5 campgrounds, 35 tent cabins

Each site has: Picnic table, fireplace

Registration: By entrance; reserve by phone, (800) 444-7275, or online, www.reserveamerica.com; for tent cabin reservations phone (800) 874-8368

Facilities: Water, flush toilets, showers, wood for sale

Parking: At individual site

Fee: $10; $8.65 nonrefundable reservation fee

Elevation: 1,000 feet

Restrictions:

Pets—On leash only; $1 fee

Fires—In fireplace

Vehicles—RVs up to 30 feet, trailers up to 27 feet

Other—2 week stay limit; 8 people per site; reservations on holidays and summer weekends recommended

BUTANO STATE PARK

near Pescadero

Drive along the windswept coast and turn inland along country roads baked golden in the sun. Turn up the canyon drained by Little Butano Creek and suddenly you are in a redwood rain forest—what an enchanted spot! Look for pygmy nuthatches, winter wrens, chickadees, banana slugs, and newts under the redwoods, Doug fir, tan oak, maple, and ferns. This is prime camping, and most folks don't even know it's here. According to Native American lore, *butano* means "a gathering place for friendly visits," and that's the vibe in Butano State Park.

The campground is up the canyon where the forest grows the thickest. Look for sites 22 through 39—these are the tent-only walk-in sites. At most, the walk is about 30 yards. The trees are so tall, the forest so still that camping here is like pitching a tent in a cathedral. The pitches are soft and spongy—although by fall there is a soft, red grit, so bring a drop cloth to clean your feet before entering your tent. The huge trees moderate the heat in the summer and the cold in the winter. Between the nearby rugged coast and these majestic trees, Butano State Park offers the best of two distinctly different worlds.

Hike up the Little Butano Creek Loop for a quick look at the park. The trail begins just below the campground. Cross the creek on footbridges and look for trillium, oxalis, and forget-me-not. In the spring,

CAMPGROUND RATINGS

Beauty:	★★★★★
Site privacy:	★★★
Site spaciousness:	★★★★
Quiet:	★★★★★
Security:	★★★★★
Cleanliness/upkeep:	★★★★

Butano State Park Campground is quiet as a church, but there is a carnival of outdoor activities around the campground.

look for baby newts. At a junction, stay below with the creek. The paths soon come together and climb through the maples. About a mile out, either cross the creek and return to the campground via an access road, or retrace your route.

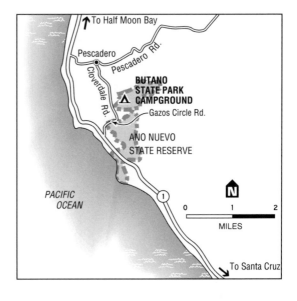

A slightly longer walk is the Jackson Flats–Six Bridges Hike. Pick this hike up down below the picnic area by the entrance booth. Head up a ridge through Doug fir, madrone, and poison oak (don't touch). After a rain, look for chanterelle mushrooms (don't pick). After a mile and a half, look for a cattail marsh on your left before entering old-growth redwoods at two miles. This is a good place to turn around. On the way back, one option is to take the Mill Ox Trail on the left and head back to the park road—go left uphill to the campground.

To visit the beach, go left on Cloverdale Road and down Gazos Creek Road to Highway 1. Go across the highway and into the Gazos Creek Access parking lot. This is a pretty little beach below Gazos, Whitehouse, and Cascade Canyons. Alternately, you can continue south exactly 1 mile. Park, and walk over the dunes to the ocean. Now, this is a great beach, with a protected cove at the south end and tidepools at the north end. A local, a professor at U.C. Santa Cruz, showed me this beach and swore me to secrecy. Ha!

A little farther south find Año Nuevo State Reserve. This is truly an incredible experience. Northern elephant seals use Año Nuevo as a rookery. Spot the island and its abandoned buildings. This used to be a lighthouse facility, and folks who lived there often chased 2,000-pound elephant seals out of the kitchen garden and sometimes found them sliding down the halls of the house.

During breeding season, between December and March, male elephant seals as big as VW bugs fight *mano a mano* for the ladies' favors. To see this spectacle, you have to go on a ranger-guided walk. You have to make reservations in advance—as early as October. Phone (650) 879-0227 for a spot. Any other time, just hiking around the reserve is wonderful. The pond is great for birdwatching—waves of different birds pass through. The beach area is pristine and protected (careful of the rips), and the Visitor Center has a fine exhibit in an old barn—once part of the Steele Brothers Dairy Farm.

Another good trip is over to Pescadero, which has the only gasoline around these parts. In the store by the pumps is a new Mexican restaurant. I talked to a California firefighter who swore by it. I tasted a homemade tamale—Olé!

For more traditional Pescadero pick up fried artichokes from Toni's Greek and American Restaurant, then drive a mile or so up Pescadero Road to the Phipps Ranch picnic tables to tuck into the chokes and drink beer from Muzzi's Market in Pescadero. Phipps is a much beloved petting zoo/U-pick farm—good strawberries. For seafood, drive up to nearby Half Moon Bay to the fish market and take your purchase back to the campground. For such a sleepy-looking stretch of coast here, there's plenty to do around Butano State Park.

To get there: from Half Moon Bay, drive 15 miles south on Highway 1 to Pescadero Road on the left. Go east on Pescadero Road, past the town of Pescadero. Go right on Cloverdale Road. The park entrance is 3 miles on the left.

KEY INFORMATION

Butano State Park
Box 3
1500 Cloverdale Road
Pescadero, CA 94515

Operated by: California Department of Parks and Recreation

Information: (650) 879-2040, (650) 330-6300; http://parks.ca.gov

Open: All year

Individual sites: 18 sites for tents only, 21 sites for tents or RVs

Each site has: Picnic table, fireplace

Registration: By entrance; reserve by phone, (800) 444-7275, or online, www.reserveamerica.com

Facilities: Water, vault toilets

Parking: At individual site

Fee: $12; $8.65 nonrefundable reservation fee

Elevation: 400 feet

Restrictions:

Pets—On leash only; $1 fee

Fires—In fireplace

Vehicles—RVs up to 27 feet, trailers up to 24 feet

Other—Reservations required on holidays and recommended for summer weekends

CASTLE CRAGS STATE PARK

near Dunsmuir

Everywhere, people love Castle Crags State Park. The guy at the dry cleaner, the waitress at the sushi restaurant—everybody likes Castle Crags. It's like a cult thing, I thought.

"No way I'll ever camp at Castle Crags," I always said. "I don't camp next to Interstate 5." One day, it was either camp in Castle Crags State Park or get a motel. We camped. The next day we went hiking. Now I'm one of those cult guys who goes around telling total strangers how much I love Castle Crags State Park and how they have to go camp there.

What an unusual place in a land of unusual places! Now I understand. It isn't Castle Crags' fault that I-5 runs by its front door. It's destiny. It was no accident the Native American trail ran by what now is called the Sacramento River—it's a natural highway—and their trail was turned into a stagecoach road, and a railroad, and then an interstate. You have to go by Castle Crags. It's at a sacred junction (no wonder the Native Americans fought to try to keep the miners out of here).

So I don't mind hearing the roar of tires on the interstate as I sleep in my beautifully conceived campsite in Castle Crags State Park. After a while, the traffic sounds like the sea, and it is strangely comforting. I don't mind crossing under the railroad and the interstate to access the Sacramento River and the River Trail.

CAMPGROUND RATINGS

Beauty:	★★★★
Site privacy:	★★★
Site spaciousness:	★★★★
Quiet:	★
Security:	★★★★★
Cleanliness/upkeep:	★★★★

Join the cult of people who adore Castle Crags State Park. Come for easy access camping and some spectacular hiking.

And, after you head up into the, dogwoods, pines, oaks, cedars, and firs—see the orchids, columbine, azaleas, and tiger lilies in the summer sun—after you climb up your first steep slope and catch a glimpse of Mount Shasta one way and those brooding granite spires called Castle Crags the other, you'll forget all about I-5. Believe me.

This campground has showers. Hot showers. I have a suspicion: is the cult of Castle Crag lovers just worn-out Pacific Crest Trail

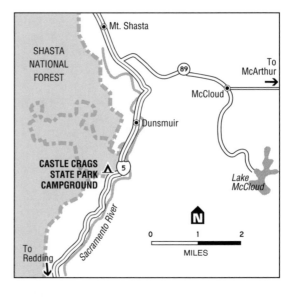

hikers in need of a hot shower? Because the PCT runs right through the park at the base of the Crags. The campsite loops are cunningly done—the trademark of the CCC boys in the 1930s who did all the work. There's a decent store right off the Castle Crags freeway exit, so you can zip down right before dinner and buy the mustard you forgot to bring for the hot dogs. I read notices that Castle Crags State Park was in bear country. But the campground garbage cans were the ordinary galvanized variety with trash liners. Why, even a baby bear would play football with a garbage can like this. I queried another camper and she said she'd been coming to Castle Crags for ten years (clearly another cult member) and had never seen a bear.

Good hiking is right in the park. Go up the narrow access road to the Vista Point (don't neglect to saunter up and take a peek). What an incredible view of Shasta, Castle Dome, Castle Crags, Gray Rocks, and Flume Ridge. Take the Crags/Indian Springs Trail. This hiking trail climbs 2 miles to Indian Springs, or 2.7 miles to the base of the Crags and Castle Dome. Head west on the trail, and soon you'll pass the Pacific Crest Trail. Keep going uphill. Past a rise of black oak, you get into evergreens. Enter Castle Crags Wilderness about a mile out and keep climbing. Soon, see Crags, Castle Dome, and Gray Rocks through the vegetation. About 2 miles out, a trail goes 1,000 yards or so to the left to Indian Springs—mossy, surrounded by cedars. Or, go right to Castle Dome.

Keep climbing on the Castle Dome Trail. It's worth it. You soon get into granite country. See Castle Dome, Mount Shasta, and the Sacramento River below. When you reach Castle Dome, keep going left until the gap in the rock where you can look down at the vertical granite. What an incredible view!

Back at camp, stretch your legs on the Indian Creek Trail. This is a breather. It's a 1-mile interpretive loop with 29 stations, and it's fairly interesting. Then take the Riverside Trail in the morning (ignore the blast of the semis barreling down the hill). Find the suspension bridge that gets you under the interstate and railroad into the park's Soda Springs area, and head left after the footbridge across Fall Creek. The fishing is good up here (having recovered from the infamous chemical railway spill of a few years ago). I saw lots of decent swimming holes and went out and waded around. This is another of Castle Crags' blessings—the swimming, which when combined with the campsites' cool, shaded mien, makes summer camping here enjoyable.

Besides the obvious drive up Mount Shasta, another good day trip is up to Castle Lake—a classic glacial cirque lake with high granite cliffs and sun-warmed rocks. Just take I-5 north to the town of Mt. Shasta. Go west, then immediately south to the end of Castle Lake Road The route is well signed.

KEY INFORMATION

Castle Crags State Park
P.O. Box 80
Castella, CA 96017-0080

Operated by: California Department of Parks and Recreation

Information: (530) 235-2684 or (530) 225-2065; http://parks.ca.gov

Open: All year

Individual sites: 76 developed sites: 32 for 18 ft.-RVs; 5 for 21 ft.-RVs; 3 for 27 ft.-RVs; 20 sites for tents only; 6 environmental

Each site has: Picnic table, fireplace, bear food locker

Registration: By entrance; reserrve by phone, (800) 444-7275, or online, www.reserveamerica.com

Facilities: Water, flush toilets, hot showers, wood for sale

Parking: At individual site

Fee: $16; $8.65 nonrefundable reservation fee

Elevation: 2,100 feet

Restrictions:

Pets—On leash only; $1 fee

Fires—In fireplace

Vehicles—RVs up to 27 feet, trailers up to 21 feet

Other—Reservations in the summer recommended; 15-day stay limit

To get there: from Dunsmuir, drive 6 miles south on I-5 to the campground, following the signs.

DILLON CREEK CAMPGROUND

Klamath National Forest, near Somes Bar

All rangers tell you Dillon Creek Campground is a good campground. "Ah, Dillon," the rangers say, and smile. "The river down there is nice." Rangers love Dillon because it is a model campground. The campground host's trailer sits right at the entrance to where the Dillon campsites file back along the hill. And, by Highway 96, Dillon is easy to patrol. I spoke to the campground host who said, "We had an unruly bear here once and I called for help on my mobile phone. The law was here in ten minutes." Did they arrest the bear? I forgot to ask.

A steep trail leads down to Dillon Creek, where there is one great swimming hole near the campground as well as dozens of more secluded ones upstream. Although Dillon Creek can flow ferociously in the spring flood, the current does not present the danger of the mighty Klamath that flows right across Highway 89 from Dillon, where everybody goes for salmon and the famous steelhead.

Beginning in the fall, the name of the game here is steelhead. For fishermen, this means the Klamath River in the winter, cold nights around a smoky campfire telling fish stories, and that one hard bite on the line that can only mean steelhead! What's a steelhead?

Steelhead are a kind of rainbow trout. Like salmon, steelhead spend some of their lives in the ocean, feeding and growing

CAMPGROUND RATINGS

Beauty: ★★★★★
Site privacy: ★★★★
Site spaciousness: ★★★
Quiet: ★★★
Security: ★★★★★
Cleanliness/upkeep: ★★★★

Good steelhead fishing. Great swimming hole. Right in the middle of the best river rafting.

faster than their exclusively freshwater cousins, rainbow trout, then head up rivers like the Klamath to spawn. Steelhead average 10 pounds (some grow to 20 or more). Unlike salmon, steelhead do not die after spawning. They can come back two or three times to spawn again.

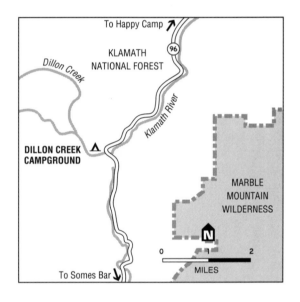

Steelhead and salmon look mostly alike. Steelhead have 9 to 12 bones or rays in their anal fin, and salmon have 13 to 19. (The anal fin is the bottom fin in front of the tail and behind the vent.) Steelhead have small, round, black spots on their back, and salmon have larger, irregular spots and lack the broad red stripe the steelhead get after being in freshwater for a while.

Peak months for catching big steelhead are January, February, and March. But littler ones (half-pounders) come into the Klamath in the spring and spend summer in big river pools before spawning in the fall rains. And other little guys and some big mothers will come into the Klamath as early as August. How you fish steelhead depends on how the run is—and how your luck is. Once you hook a steelhead, it takes skill to land one, for steelhead are acrobatic, hard-fighting fish. Good luck! Of course, to decrease the odds, ask around in Happy Camp (don't you just love the name of that town!) for a good fishing guide.

Last time I was in Dillon was September 1996, and the fall run of steelhead had not arrived. The campground host told me anglers were catching steelhead down near Somes Bar. Only mildly disappointed, we put on our water shoes and went down to the swimming hole. It was nice and hot. We had good fun working our way up Dillon Creek River, checking things out. We took a picnic, found a nice warm rock next to a clear pool, and hung out for the afternoon.

The next day, we found a trail that ran up the north side of Dillon Creek, and followed it up a mile or so. Later I heard that this trail is used by the Fish and Game people who hike up to where Dillon Creek forks to do a fish count. South of the campground entrance, Forest Service Road 13N35 heads up the shoulder of Dillon Mountain (4,679 feet). We hiked it until it got too steep and the sun got too hot.

There is also a trail that heads up the mountain behind the campground, but I couldn't find anyone who knew where it went. Basically, by the time you get as far out in the woods as Dillon Creek Campground, folks don't spend much time marking trails. And, since this is rugged individualist country—land of tacked-together shacks tied to the Klamath River bank with rusty cables, and pot plantations among the redwoods—it is not a healthy idea to lunge blindly off into the woods. You might end up fertilizer. Try to stick to the river bank and to semiofficial trails or roads.

For adventure, try river rafting. Happy Camp is full of experienced outfits happy to take you down the river. I recommend going with an outfit your first couple of times out before trying anything hasty. Proper equipment is a must; a helmet and life jacket can make a huge difference when you, your spouse, or your kid are dumped suddenly into the rapids.

Happy Camp (as well as having good hamburgers at the western-style bar/cafe in town) has a good supermarket. I saw fliers up in town for folks who will take you gold panning and horseback riding. The Happy Camp Ranger Station has all the details. This little town seems friendly as well as happy.

KEY INFORMATION

Dillon Creek Campground, Klamath National Forest
Ukonom Ranger District
P.O. Drawer 410
Orleans, CA 95556-0410

Operated by: U.S. Forest Service

Information: (530) 627-3291; www.r5.fs.fed.us/klamath

Open: May to October

Individual sites: 10 sites for tents only, 11 sites for RVs

Each site has: Picnic table, fireplace

Registration: By entrance

Facilities: Water, vault toilets

Parking: At individual site

Fee: $9 first car, additional car $5; group rate (4 cars) $18

Elevation: 800 feet

Restrictions:

Pets—On leash only

Fires—In fireplace

Vehicles—No trailers over 22 feet

Other—Check weather conditions and water availabilty

To get there: from Somes Bar, drive 15 miles north on Highway 96. Or, drive 25 miles south of Happy Camp on Highway 96.

EAGLE CREEK CAMPGROUND

Shasta–Trinity National Forest, near Trinity Center

This is a pretty little campground. It is right on the Trinity River for convenient fishing. It is easy to get to. The only other campgrounds nearby are on the Clair Engle (Trinity) Lake where the water level is quixotic at best—the lakeshore often looks like future world when the water level is reduced for power generation and irrigation. But the real reason to come here is the Trinity Alps.

On the way to Eagle Creek Campground, you cross an old-style bridge (stop on the bridge and look down into the river below—you can see down through the grate and you feel like you are walking on air). Head right for a mile or so to Eagle Creek Campground on the right. The campsites are set in a pined hummock a few hundred yards from the river. The pitches are soft and needled; most of the sites are shaded and cool. Only four of the sites face the river, where the boulders on the banks show white as bones in the light, and the rush of the water covers the occasional rumble of a lumber truck on Highway 3.

Look up at the Trinity Alps from Eagle Creek Campground. Do they look familiar? If you know the Sierra Nevada, then the Trinity Alps should look familiar because the two mountain ranges are more than kissing cousins—they are separate parts of a single dismembered mountain range. Rocks along the southern edge of the Trinities match those on the northern

CAMPGROUND RATINGS

Beauty:	★★★★
Site privacy:	★★★★★
Site spaciousness:	★★★★★
Quiet:	★★★
Security:	★★
Cleanliness/upkeep:	★★★★

Come camp at Eagle Creek Campground and see the fabulous Trinity Alps. Bring a fishing rod and a mountain bike if you can.

end of the Sierra Nevada like matching parts of a torn dollar bill. Each major belt of rock and fault in one has its match in the other. Somehow a single mountain range broke in two pieces, which moved about 60 miles apart. All this happened about 140 million years ago, when the ranges were young. Nobody knows exactly how, but the mother range bent and broke before drifting apart to form the Sierra Nevada and the Trinity Alps.

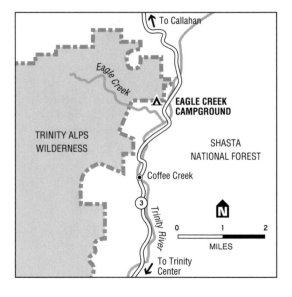

The fishing done up here is mostly for trout. A good rule of thumb is the farther you hike in, the better the fishing will be. Anywhere close to the road gets fished big time—folks take the larger fish and leave the smaller ones. So, in the end, close to the road you get lots of small, wily fish. Hike in and you get the big dumb ones ready for the skillet. Now, steelhead is a different matter. The best steelhead fishing is found between the Lewiston Bridge and Douglas City. Best to ask advice locally—the natives do want you to catch fish, come back, and spend more tourist dollars.

Bring a mountain bike if you can. There is a myriad of small roads and logging roads to ride. Right across from the campground are Ramshorn Creek Road and North Fork Road. Or ride south of the campground past Eagle Creek Ranch and access the logging roads to the west. Or head down Highway 3, and ride west up Coffee Creek Road. Some enthusiastic cyclers camping next to us at Eagle Creek Campground rode down East Side Road into Jackass Springs Campground to have lunch and a swim.

You'll need some experience to hike the Trinity Alps, which tend to go straight up the first 5 or so miles. A little conditioning at home will save you from leaden-thigh malaise the first day out. Take it really easy the first day so you don't blow yourself out. The hike up to nearby Big Bear Lake is a good starter if you go slowly. Go out of Eagle Creek Campground and turn left on Highway 3. A couple miles up you'll see the turnoff for the Bear Creek Parking Area and the trailhead at the north end of the Bear Creek Loop.

The hike in is about 3 miles. You gain 2,800 feet, but the hike isn't that fierce. We hiked with an old dog and he didn't seem too put out. Right from the beginning, up through the Doug fir and oak, this is a pretty hike. You cross a bridge over Bear Creek, and pretty soon you can see the white granite peaks on the south side of the creek. See the glacial cirque up high—this is where Little and Wee Bear Lakes sit. Keep going up Bear Creek Canyon into the hemlock, fir, and white pine, then the trail cuts down by the creek through alder and coffeeberry (Native Americans used this plant's bark to make medicine). Head up the last rock face past the waterfall to Big Bear Lake itself. This is a classic Trinity Alps lake, with granite rising into spires around the deep blue water. What a beautiful spot!

Another good hike (though harder to access) is the 2-mile stroll to Stoddard Lake, with its lodgepole-pined shores and pretty meadows. Turn right out of Eagle Creek Campground and drive about 6 or 7 miles on very rough but passable Forest Service Road 38N27 to the trailhead. The trail swings up over the lake past Stoddard meadow and cabin and drops down to the water.

Eagle Creek Campground is open all year—but count on snow by Thanksgiving. Also, the rangers cut off the water October 31.

KEY INFORMATION

Eagle Creek Campground, Shasta–Trinity National Forest
Forest Supervisor
2400 Washington Avenue
Redding, CA 96001

Operated by: U.S. Forest Service

Information: (530) 246-5222, (530) 623-2121; www.r5.fs.fed.us/ shastatrinity

Open: May through October

Individual sites: 17 sites for tents and RVs

Each site has: Picnic table, fireplace

Registration: By entrance

Facilities: Water, vault toilets

Parking: At individual site

Fee: $8 (free after October 31 when water is shut off)

Elevation: 2,800 feet

Restrictions:

Pets—On leash only

Fires—In fireplace

Vehicles—Trailers up to 27 feet

Other—Check weather conditions and water availabilty; 14-day stay limit

To get there, drive 16 miles north of Trinity Center (last good food shop) on Highway 3. See sign on left, cross bridge, and go right. Drive 1 mile to campground entrance.

THE COAST

ELK PRAIRIE CAMPGROUND

Prairie Creek Redwoods State Park, near Orick

This pretty campground is perfect for families. Just off Highway 101, Elk Prairie Campground has all the amenities—flush toilets, hot showers, secluded campsites set off in redwoods and maples, and a meadow full of children-pleasing wapiti, otherwise known as elk. These huge animals, *Cervus elaphus* (or Roosevelt elk in honor of Teddy, the president who helped protect them), are instant crowd pleasers. Cars come to screeching halts on Highway 101 when elk appear beside the road. Kids are fascinated by their huge antlers. The baby elk melt anyone's heart.

The trails are many and easy—and free of poison oak! A few miles away (by car or foot) is the most beautiful, most secluded sandy beach in all of California. Orick, a few miles to the south, has all the redwood burls the world could ever desire, groceries, and brunches at Rolf's Park Cafe—a German schnitzel house featuring elk steak.

The absolute best time to come is in September and October when the sun shines. Summer is warmer, but expect some fog and be prepared to dress for it. Spring has rainy spells but also wildflowers.

Winter is a bear, and unless you arrive between huge storms, prepare to be wet—some folks love it this way. Seal the seams on your tent. The way it rains up here, water will come up through untreated seams to make a lap pool on the floor of your tent. Bring a garden trowel to ditch

CAMPGROUND RATINGS

Beauty:	★★★★★
Site privacy:	★★★★★
Site spaciousness:	★★★
Quiet:	★★★
Security:	★★★★★
Cleanliness/upkeep:	★★★★★

Elk Prairie Campground is good for a summer family vacation. There are the redwoods, the beach, and the elk to amuse the kids.

around the tent and a good drop cloth to lay under the tent. Fold the sides of the drop cloth up under the tent, so the water won't pool between the tent floor and the drop cloth. Also bring good books and playing cards.

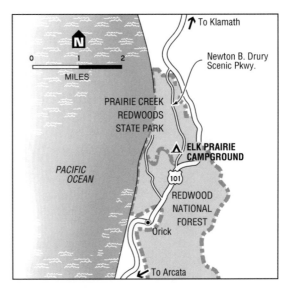

The elk don't mind the wet. They're just glad not to be hunted to near extermination for their meat, hide, and upper canine teeth. Once these elk ranged over most of the continent—from the Berkshires in western Massachusetts to southern New Mexico. By 1912 the elk herd was down to about 15 elk. They made their last stand here in Prairie Creek Redwoods State Park.

Elk love elk. Very gregarious, elk band together even at the risk of running out of pasture. Known for their huge, intimidating antlers, bull elk are paper tigers. The antlers seem to be mostly show. When elk fight, they strike with their front feet and use the antlers for a chopping, downward motion. Most important for the bull elk is his bugle—the low note rising a full octave to a sweet, mellow crescendo, dropping by degrees to the first note, then a few coughing grunts. The Elk bulls here are big bark and little bite. Of course, humanoids should not approach elk or get in their way.

Listen to AM radio 1610 while in the park. This is elk locale news and will tell you where the herd is. A good elk-spotting hike is around Elk Prairie. Bring binoculars. A little over 2 miles, the loop should take a little over an hour. Start near campsite 67 and follow the trail south through Sitka spruce and alder. Cross a little stream, then head into the open prairie. At a break in the fence, head across the prairie to the parkway, cross it, and pick up the trail on the other side. This trail will parallel the parkway. Look for signs of elk—tracks, bark rubbed off, tender shoots eaten, elk wallows—and the elk herd itself. Keep going until you reach a junction with the Rhododendron and Cathedral Trees Trail. Go left and circle back to the campground, going under the parkway by the kiosk and Visitor Center.

Another good hike is down to Fern Canyon and the beach via the James Irvine Trail. This is a day hike, about 8 miles round-trip, so take water and food. To pick up the James Irvine Trail, take the Nature Trail by the Visitor Center, cross Prairie Creek on a bridge, and continue past the start of the Prairie Creek Trail until you see the James Irvine Trail. The trail follows Godwood Creek through virgin redwood, Sitka spruce, Doug fir, and hemlock. At almost 3 miles you cross a bridge over the headwater of Home Creek. Follow Home Creek down into Fern Canyon. Gold Bluffs Beach is just beyond. Lots of folks drive through the park to visit Fern Canyon.

Look out for the famous banana slug, bright yellow and about six inches long. They crawl around conspicuously and like to eat all sorts of forest litter and debris. So famous indeed, the slug has been proposed as the California state mollusk. They are hermaphrodites and have penises as long as their bodies. When they mate, they impregnate each other—thus neatly opting out of the war between the sexes. Camp in August and attend the official Banana Slug Derby!

To get there: from Orick, drive 6 miles north on Highway 101. Go left on the Newton B. Drury Scenic Parkway and left again into Elk Prairie Campground.

KEY INFORMATION

Elk Prairie Campground
Prairie Creek Redwoods
State Park
Orick, CA 95555

Operated by: California Department of Parks and Recreation

Information: (707) 464-6101 ext. 5301; http://parks.ca.gov

Open: All year

Individual sites: 71 sites for tents or RVs; 3 wheelchair accessible

Each site has: Picnic table, fire ring

Registration: By entrance; reserve by phone, (800) 444-7275, or online, www.reserveamerica.com

Facilities: Water, flush toilets, showers, wood for sale

Parking: At individual site

Fee: $12; $8.65 nonrefundable reservation fee

Elevation: 150 feet

Restrictions:

Pets—On leash only

Fires—In fire ring

Vehicles—RVs up to 27 feet, trailers up to 24 feet

Other—Reservations on holidays and summer weekends recommended

COAST

GOLD BLUFFS BEACH CAMPGROUND

Prairie Creek Redwoods State Park, near Orick

Gold Bluffs Beach has to be the prettiest sand beach in California. Steep sandstone cliffs rise up to more eroded cliffs spiked with towering Sitka spruce. The salt and pepper sand beach stretches as far as the eye can see in both directions. There's a sea mist kicked up by the surf that bathes the scene with billowing white. The waves break far out and slowly comb to shore. What an incredible beach!

And the Gold Bluffs Beach Campground is the best beach campground on the California coast. There are 25 sites, available on a first come, first served basis and all in the dunes a hundred yards back from the beach. Some sites have railroad-tie wind shelters. Behind you are the wildflowered bluffs, ahead a couple thousand miles of blue water—and Hawaii. Surf fish for perch, and dip for smelt at night.

Wind scours the sand. The beach and the campground are always clean, by morning pristine—the footprints and debris of the day before blown away in the night. The facilities are also clean, and the solar showers are hot if the sun shines. The beach is nice and level, perfect for hiking and beach combing. The mist keeps the sun from being too hot, and that sea breeze always blows sweet in your face. Nothing could be more perfect—except for the weather.

Don't expect great weather on Gold Bluffs Beach unless you come in September or October, which are the premium

CAMPGROUND RATINGS

Beauty:	★★★★★
Site privacy:	★★★
Site spaciousness:	★★★
Quiet:	★★★★★
Security:	★★★★★
Cleanliness/upkeep:	★★★★★

Gold Bluffs Beach Campground has the prettiest, most remote beach camping in California. The hiking and surf fishing are fantastic.

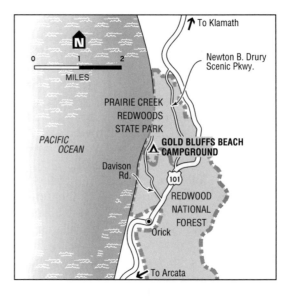

weather months in this part of the world. From October to April, Gold Bluffs Beach gets a ton of rain. Of course, rain here is cosmic symphonics—the clouds billow, blacken, and boil across the sky; the wind brings rain slashing sideways into the sand; and the surf churns up gray to reflect the sky. Suddenly you know why your tent is double-stitched, and thank the Lord you remembered to seal your seams against the wet. It rains. Just south of here, the Lost Coast can get up to 200 inches of rain yearly. Think about it. That's 16 feet of water—10 feet over the average guy's head!

April and May are windy with some rainstorms, and the wildflowers start growing like crazy on the bluffs. Look for Indian paintbrush, cow parsnip, iris, and lupine. In June, July, and August expect hot, sunny summer days alternating with thick fog. But September and October are heaven, when the beach is at its most beautiful, the bluffs are cooked gold, and the sea is a deep green.

There is no cover at the campground, so think about how to manage the sun and wind. Bring big hats and lots of sunblock, and try to improvise shade. With rope and a sturdy tarp, one can usually arrange makeshift shade. Kelty sells a sunshade for about $150 that looks like a grounded kite. We used it once, and it held up agreeably to less-than-hurricane winds, when most other dining canopies would have blown halfway to Kansas. I think the most portable arrangement is a sombrero and a cheap sun umbrella that clamps on to your aluminum chair (umbrellas can be found next to the aluminum chairs in your favorite discount store).

The first folks here were the Yurok Indians, who didn't have these amenities. They lived in a village by the lagoon, just south of where Davison Road hits the beach. Then came the gold miners in 1850, who found flecks of gold mixed with the gray-and-black sand at Gold Bluffs Beach. Miners flooded the area and were terribly disappointed when they discovered that the gold was bound so tightly to the sand that it had to be extracted with quicksilver sluice boxes. And, the gold-bearing sand was only available when waves crashed against the bluff and dislodged big chunks of the bank. Most of the miners fled for other diggin's.

A few stayed and used mules to carry the sand ore up to the bluffs. Apparently, the mule trips were timed so the animals could avoid waves and reach their destination dry. In those days, the beach was much narrower than now. As the beach widened, the waves stopped cutting away at the bluff, and all mining stopped. Still, look above Carruther's Cove for the flume that cuts across the hillside. On the knoll above Major Creek there are still some boards left from Chapman's Union Gold Bluff Mine.

Hiking here is on the beach and on the trails heading east to Elk Prairie Campground. The short loop around Fern Canyon is a don't-miss jaunt. With 50-foot walls of ferns, Fern Canyon sits a couple miles north of Gold Bluffs Beach Campground. The most common fern here is the five-finger fern, a relative of the maidenhair fern. The Yuroks gathered these ferns for the black stems they wove into their incredible baskets. Look for the banana slug and the omnivorous Pacific giant salamander. Also, look for winter wrens, the water ouzel, and great blue heron.

KEY INFORMATION

Gold Bluffs Beach Campground
Prairie Creek Redwoods State Park
Orick, CA 95555
Operated by: California Department of Parks and Recreation

Information: (707) 464-6101 ext. 5301; http://parks.ca.gov

Open: All year

Individual sites: 25 sites for tents or small RVs

Each site has: Picnic table, fireplace, bear box

Registration: By entrance; reserve by phone, (800) 444-7275, or online, www.reserveamerica.com

Facilities: Water, flush toilets, solar showers

Parking: At individual site

Fee: $12; $8.65 nonrefundable reservation fee

Elevation: 10 feet

Restrictions:

Pets—On leash only; $1 fee

Fires—In fireplace

Vehicles—RVs up to 20 feet, no trailers

Other—Store food in bear boxes; canoeing requires a permit

To get there: from Orick, go 3 miles north on Highway 101 to Davison Road on the left. Go 4 miles on Davison Road to Gold Bluffs Beach Campground. Drive carefully; the road is narrow, unpaved, and slippery when wet.

THE COAST

IDLEWILD CAMPGROUND

Klamath National Forest, near Sawyers Bar

There are two ways to get into Idlewild Campground, and they both are beautiful. One is over the Etna-Salmon Mountain Summit from Etna (elevation: 5,958 feet), and though your car will cough, your spirit will soar like an eagle as you look out over the Marble Mountain Wilderness. The other way is hellaciously beautiful—the hairy but sublime drive up from Somes Bar or Callahan, through Forks of Salmon, past rickety Sawyers Bar, to Idlewild Campground. Drive carefully. Keep your lights on, your car window rolled down to listen for other traffic, and blow your horn as you go around the thousands of blind curves. This has to be the most beautiful drive in California. But, as you know from the movies (and real life), beauty can be perilous. Never mind, hang on to the wheel, tempt fate, and pray you don't meet the runaway logging truck from Valhalla.

In direct contrast with the drive in, Idlewild Campground is about as restful as a place can be. Where the North Fork Salmon River wraps around, the sound of the rushing water lulls you into the big sleep. Our first night at Idlewild we were out for 12 hours. The campground is old-fashioned—the sites are mostly private and nicely spread out. We had an old-style Forest Service outdoor stove with an iron griddle, which reminded me of camping in the 1950s—sausages, bacon, flapjacks, and eggs

CAMPGROUND RATINGS

Beauty:	★★★★★
Site privacy:	★★★★★
Site spaciousness:	★★★★★
Quiet:	★★★★
Security:	★★★
Cleanliness/upkeep:	★★★★

A tranquil camp with great fishing, swimming, bicycling, and hiking. The best in the West.

frying on the iron in the morning and fried trout with hush puppies at night. The drinking water is cold and clean.

At night, we hiked along the deserted Sawyers Bar Road. The trees open up along the road, so you can see the stars and always find your way back to camp. I kept getting déjà vu. Are we in the Sierra Nevada?

The answer is yes. These mountains are an extension of the Sierra Nevada—the connecting area was buried many moons ago by lava

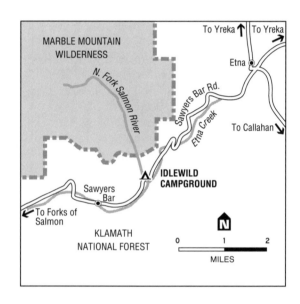

flows from the southern Cascades. Glaciers rolled down, shaping the granite into jagged peaks and carved U-shaped valleys, leaving moraines, cirques, and lakes. Consequently, this area feels like the Sierra Nevada.

There's gold, too. As you drive up Sawyers Bar Road, see all the No Trespassing signs for the various rawhide gold mines. Respect the signs. This is also pot plantation area, and the farming locals might shoot first and ask questions afterwards. Just stick to roads and the official trails, and don't go plunging blindly into the woods.

Bring fishing gear. The fishing around here for steelhead and salmon is world famous. In fact, last time I was here, in September, the fishing was so good that there was no fishing at all. Fish and Game shut the Salmon River down because fishing was so good it was depleting the fish stock. Call the Ranger Station before you come, and get the word on what's hot and where it's hot, and what the locals are using on the end of their lines.

Bicycling is superb here as well. Head downstream past Sawyers Bar to Forks of Salmon, keeping in mind you have to climb about 1,000 feet to come back to the campground. Cycling, you can hear the cars and trucks coming so you can take cover. It's easy, too, to pull over, park your bike, and head down to the river. For organized trips, there are outfits (the Ranger Station has their phone numbers) working out of Cecilville that offer bicycle tours and kayak trips down the river.

Right by Idlewild Campground is the Mule Creek Bridge Trailhead. Go out of the campground and immediately turn right on Forest Service Road 41N37. Go 2.3 miles past some cabins and find the trailhead on your right (notice good dispersed camping spots by the river). The first 10 miles is great, no-sweat hiking. It is fairly flat—full of wonderful places for swimming, fishing, and picnicking. Look at the trees down by the river—alder, maple, cottonwood, and willow. And the woods are full of Doug fir, oak, sugar pine, incense cedar, ponderosa pine, and madrona. In September, all the berries were ready to be picked. They all looked like blackberries to me, but another hiker identified them as huckleberries and thimbleberries. I kept looking out for hungry bears but didn't see any sign.

We never got there, but Lake of the Island's turnoff is about 8 miles along the trail. You cross the river and head 2 miles up to 13-acre Lake of the Island, a 25-foot-deep pool filled with brook and rainbow trout. Since I never made it, I only have the berry-identification hiker's account of Lake of the Island. "Yes," he said. "There is an island in the middle of Lake of the Island." He camped up there for two days and had a great time of it.

Once you see the river and take a dip at night in the pools, you'll want to stay forever. If you get a hankering for Thai food, jump in your ancient flivver and fly over to Sengthon's at 434 Main Street in Etna.

KEY INFORMATION

Idlewild Campground, Klamath National Forest
Salmon River Ranger District
11263 N. Highway 3
Fort Jones, CA 96032-9702

Operated by: U.S. Forest Service

Information: (530) 468-5351, (530) 467-5757; TDD (530) 468-2783; www.rs.fs.fed.us/klamath

Open: May through November (phone ahead to confirm)

Individual sites: 21 sites for tents and small RVs

Each site has: Picnic table, fireplace

Registration: By entrance

Facilities: Water, vault toilets

Parking: At individual site

Fee: $6

Elevation: 2,600 feet

Restrictions:

Pets—On leash only

Fires—In fireplace

Vehicles—RVs up to 22 feet

Other—Check weather conditions and water availabilty

To get there: from Etna, drive 16 miles south on Sawyers Bar Road to the campground on the right. The town of Sawyers Bar is a few miles south of Idlewild Campground.

JEDEDIAH SMITH CAMPGROUND

Jedediah Smith Redwoods State Park, east of Crescent City

By the time the road-weary camper arrives Jedediah Smith Redwoods State Park near the Oregon border, he's bound to throw up his hands and plead, "Oh, Lord, not another beautiful Redwoods State Park!"

Jedediah Smith Redwoods State Park is gorgeous. Not only does the Smith River run by the campground for unparalleled fishing, canoeing, kayaking, and swimming, but also the hiking is great. The wild Smith River National Recreational Area is next door, and the summer weather is usually nice and sunny! Jedediah Smith Campground is fortuitously far enough east to escape the cool summer fog that plagues other state parks in redwood country. Hallelujah! The kids can paddle happily around in the river (old sneakers or water shoes of some sort are a must!) while dad sits in his lawn chair by the river and casts for trout. Meanwhile, the rays of the sun will stream through the crowns of the high redwoods and splash on the ground.

Jedediah Smith Campground should really be named Sitragitum or Tcunsultum Campground for either of the two Tolowa Native American villages that were in the area, because namesake Jedediah Smith was only here less than a day in 1828 on his way to getting most of his men rubbed out in Oregon. The famous Bible-toting pathfinder, Smith, made the mistake of humiliating an Umpqua tribesman whom

CAMPGROUND RATINGS

Beauty:	★★★★★
Site privacy:	★★★
Site spaciousness:	★★★
Quiet:	★★★
Security:	★★★★★
Cleanliness/upkeep:	★★★★

Jedediah Smith is the most northern of California's beautiful Redwoods State Parks. And the sun shines through the summer fog!

they suspected of stealing an ax. Big mistake. Two days later, a hundred Umpqua warriors attacked and killed 16 of Smith's long-haired and buckskin-fringed trappers. Only Two trappers fought their way to safety. Smith just happened to be off scouting when the attack happened and heard the news from one of the survivors. Smith explored on—finally losing his hair a few years later to some Comanche by a water hole on the Arkansas River.

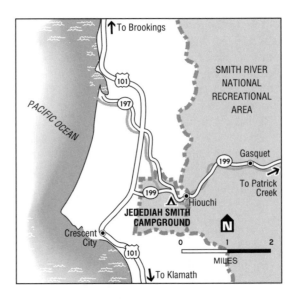

Most of the good hiking from Jedediah Smith Campground is across the Smith River. During the summer, there is a footbridge across the river to connect with the Hiouchi Trail. The footbridge is by the winter boat launch between campsites 84 and 86. The rest of the year prepare to get your feet wet. Remember, it's hard walking on all that river rock in your bare feet, so bring some water shoes. After crossing the summer bridge, or wading the river, go left for the Mill Creek Trail. The trail follows Mill Creek southeast to Howland Road and the Boy Scout Tree Road. Go right for the Simpson-Reed Discovery Trail and the Hatton Loop, which are must-see excursions. (To access them by car, just exit the Jedediah Smith Campground and drive 2 miles west on Highway 199.)

Across the highway from the Hatton Loop, the Simpson-Reed Discovery Trail is wonderfully done. Taking only about half an hour to make the loop, I learned all kinds of things about the coastal redwoods and the plants that live around them—like how to identify the redwood sorrel with its purple undersides and pink flowers, and why hemlock stands on its roots. Called the octopus tree, hemlock seeds germinate on decaying redwood logs. Their roots straddle redwood logs, which finally rot totally away, leaving the hemlock roots looking like wooden legs. I also learned that the huge redwoods come from tiny seeds—a pound of redwood seeds would start a hundred thousand trees.

If you tire of the bustle of Jedediah Smith Campground, head down to Big Flat Campground off South Fork Road for some real peace and quiet. Big Flat is in the Smith River National Recreational Area, an amazing 305,337-acre hunk of wilderness in the Six River National Forest. The campground has 30 sites, but no potable water. Sites cost $4 per night. To reach Big Flat Campground, just turn south on South Fork Road. Turn left after crossing the second bridge, and travel 12 miles on South Fork Road to French Hill Road. Turn left on French Hill Road, and go 100 feet to the Big Flat Campground entrance on the left.

The drive south on South Fork Road is sublime. The Smith River, the last wild, undammed river in California, runs through granite gorges, through rapids, down into deep pools. All along the road there are parking spots where one can leave the car and hike down to the river. (This is fine bicycling!) Most of the trails from the parking spots head for the best steelhead bank fishing.

The nearest supply from Jedediah Smith Campground is Hiouchi, a few hundred yards east. Hiouchi has a gas station, a small market, a cafe—and a decent RV park with a grass field to camp on if Jedediah Smith is packed in.

If you tire of camp grub, head down to Crescent City to the Harbor View Grotto restaurant on Citizen's Dock Road or try the Ship Ashore restaurant up in Smith River, just off Highway 101. Eat great seafood and look out over the Smith River estuary. Life can't get any better.

Jedediah Smith Redwoods State Park
4241 Kings Valley Road
Crescent City, CA 95531

Operated by: California Department of Parks and Recreation

Information: (707) 464-6101; http://parks.ca.gov

Open: All year

Individual sites: 106 sites for tents or RVs

Each site has: Picnic table, fireplace

Registration: By entrance; reserve by phone, (800) 444-7275, or online, www.reserveamerica.com

Facilities: Water, flush toilets, showers, wood for sale

Parking: At individual site

Fee: $12; $8.65 nonrefundable reservation fee

Elevation: 150 feet

Restrictions:

Pets—On leash only; $1 fee

Fires—In fireplace

Vehicles—RVs and trailers up to 30 feet

Other—Reservations on holidays and summer weekends recommended

To get there: from Crescent City, go 9 miles east on Highway 199. The Jedediah Smith Campground is on your right before you get to Hiouchi.

THE COAST

MACKERRICHER STATE PARK

Fort Bragg

What campground is by 8 miles of beach, a beautiful headland, rolling dunes, lowland forest, a freshwater lake, and hundreds of snoozing harbor seals? MacKerricher State Park Campground is cheek and jowl with all of the above. The park offers hiking, cycling, surfing, canoeing, fishing, and horseback riding. Thank Canadian-born dairy farmer Duncan MacKerricher who bought the land for $1.25 an acre back in 1868 and whose family later deeded it to the great state of California, specifying that access to the land would be free in perpetuity.

The four campground loops, East Pinewood, West Pinewood, Cleone, and Surfwood, are pretty close together. East Pinewood is closer to the road. Cleone is a little closer to Cleone Pond. Surfwood is down by the beach but near the main beach traffic. I like West Pinewood best because it is off the highway and near the Haul Road Trail and an uncrowded beach. All the sites in all the loops are wonderfully separated and private. This is a first-class campground. There are even 11 walk-in campgrounds (less than 50 yards away) in the Surfwood Loop for even more privacy. What a great park!

Even though the campsites are protected by pines, brush, and ferns, come prepared for wind and rain. Weather on the Mendocino coast is unpredictable, though the scenery is often most beautiful when the

CAMPGROUND RATINGS

Beauty: ★★★★★
Site privacy: ★★★★★
Site spaciousness: ★★★★
Quiet: ★★★
Security: ★★★★★
Cleanliness/upkeep: ★★★★

MacKerricher State Park has everything but the promise of sunny weather.

weather is inclement. Sometimes, of course, the sun will shine for months.

Cleone Pond is perfect for launching a canoe or kayak, and good, too, for trout when stocked and for some big, wary bass. The fishing here is relaxing, with the crash of the ocean waves only a sand dune away. There's a good mile walk around the pond through marsh, cattail, and bishop pine.

Take the Seal Point Trail, and hike a few hundred yards out on the walkway to Seal Rocks, where you

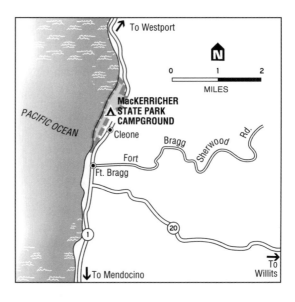

should see tons of seals sleeping like sleek dufflebags on the rocks. Remember to bring binoculars to discern their cute little whiskered faces. Check out all the pretty spots on their creamy-to-dark-brown bodies. These critters spend most of their time copping zzzzzs, but they will all dive into the water at the sign of danger (an alarm bark). They can dive to 300 feet and stay submerged up to 28 minutes. Feeding time is when the tide comes in. Sometimes they head up the rivers with the tide to eat, then haul out at low tide and snooze some more.

There is pretty good rock fishing north of Seal Rocks. Locals use squid for bait and tobacco sack weights. The fishing stores sell these little fabric tobacco sacks for next to nothing that you can fill with sand or small rocks and tie on to your line as weight. When the weight tangles up in the rocks, just give a pull and the tobacco sack weight breaks off, leaving you with your rock fish on the hook. Watch for rogue waves—the sudden big waves that come out of nowhere and threaten to suck you out to China.

It's fun, too, to go tidepooling in the rocks at low tide. Or poke-poling! Here's what you do. Wear old sneakers and swimming shorts. Get a bamboo pole and attach a fishing hook on a two-inch bit of wire to the end of the pole. Bait the hook with squid or mussels (rumors fly about the efficacy of abalone). Go around the tidepools in the shallow reef areas (best in minus tides), and stick the bait down under every rock and crevice. You'll get eels and rockfish and maybe small octopus. Serious poke-polers wear wetsuit bottoms so they can stay out longer. Bring a burlap sack for the booty.

Good bicycling awaits on the 7-mile Haul Road bicycle route that goes from the north side of Pudding Creek to the south, all the way north to the mouth of Ten-Mile River. There's also decent cycling on the Fort Bragg Sherwood Road that heads out in Fort Bragg as Oak Avenue. Great fun for everybody is the horseback riding. Ricochet Ridge Ranch in Cleone just north of the Mac-Kerricher State Park entrance has guided rides on the beach or in the redwoods for very reasonable prices.

The campgrounds are right by Fort Bragg, which promotes itself as the town "where Prosperity reigns, and where it rains prosperity." Fort Bragg (named for Braxton Bragg, a general in the Confederate Army) was first a particularly brutal Indian reservation and is now home to the Georgia-Pacific Lumber Mill. Go eat great seafood in Noyo Harbor just south of town. Try Samraat Cuisine on Main Street. A friend who served in the Peace Corps in India says he didn't have better food in Bombay.

Go to the Mendocino Coast Botanical Gardens. Best bloom is in May, but anytime has something in season. Or, ride the Skunk Train (phone (707) 964-6371) at the foot of Laurel Street. Antique railcars run 40 miles through the redwoods to Willits, crossing 30 bridges and going through 2 long tunnels.

KEY INFORMATION

MacKerricher State Park
P.O. Box 440
Mendocino, CA 95460

Operated by: California Department of Parks and Recreation

Information: (707) 937-5804; http://parks.ca.gov

Open: All year

Individual sites: 142 sites for tents or RVs, 11 walk-in sites (a 50-yard walk away)

Each site has: Picnic table, fireplace

Registration: By entrance; reserve by phone, (800) 444-7275, or online, www.reserveamerica.com

Facilities: Water, flush toilets, hot showers, wood for sale

Parking: At individual site

Fee: $12; $8.65 nonrefundable reservation fee

Elevation: 50 feet

Restrictions:

Pets—On leash only

Fires—In fireplace

Vehicles—RVs and trailers up to 35 feet

Other—Reservations in summer recommended

To get there: from Fort Bragg, go 3 miles north on Highway 1 to the MacKerricher State Park entrance on the left.

MANCHESTER STATE BEACH

Manchester

How beautiful! And, how the wind does blow! No matter what time of year, this campground is ski-jacket country. And summer can be the worst. The winds blow so hard out of the north that you want to tie your tent to the car (seriously, bring extra rope to strategically tie your tent to nearby coyote brush and ceanothus). But, when it's sunny, especially in winter or fall, Manchester Beach can melt your heart. Nowhere is the coastline so beautiful. Nowhere does the lighthouse stand so starkly against the sea and sky. And, probably, nowhere are the locals as friendly as they are here.

Manchester (with a good grocery store) is a hop, skip, and a jump from the campground. Nearby Point Arena even has a community-owned, first-run movie theater and playhouse. This country looks like the west coast of Wales, and the people feel like the Welsh—courteous, reserved, with a twinkle in their eye, and all balled up in wool sweaters against the weather.

The campground sites are nicely separated and set into the gorse for some privacy from the the chest down. Then there's the beach. Miles and miles of sandy beach, with grassy dunes and the Pacific running off into the sky. Think ruddy. With the wind off the water, your face goes quickly red, and soon you look like a native.

Take the Alder Creek Trail from the campground. Round-trip is about 4 miles,

CAMPGROUND RATINGS

Beauty:	★★★★★
Site privacy:	★★★★
Site spaciousness:	★★★★
Quiet:	★★★★★
Security:	★★★★★
Cleanliness/upkeep:	★★★★★

Windy and cold at times, Manchester State Beach Campground is always breathtakingly beautiful. Get reservations for peak times.

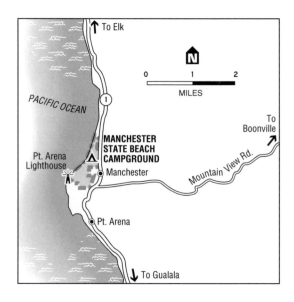

and the loop should take you around two hours. The trail starts by Park Head-quarters, goes past Lake Davis to the beach, and on north to Alder Creek, where there are birds and birds (bring binoculars) around the lagoon. Look for the whistling swan. Unlike the mute swan, the whistlers hold their neck straight and bill level, and some-times show a bright yellow spot on their black bill. The immature swan is a light gray-brown. Since the whistler is our most com-mon swan, the chances that the swans you see in the lagoon are whistlers are pretty good. The "whistle" of the whistling swan comes from that ethereal sound the swans make when they are flying to and from the Arctic, where they nest. These swans have a 7-foot wingspan and weigh up to 20 pounds—and they need all of it for the journey. They come all that way to hang out in the "mild" Manchester Beach weather for the winter. In addition to swans, look for pelicans, godwits, killdeer, and surf scoters (a variety of sea duck).

Peaceful Alder Creek used to be famous for its "grizz"—the huge California bears that hung out around here. Imagine coming around a curve in Alder Creek and running into a mammoth grumpy grizzly bear. That would thin out the tourist herd. Fortunately for us, the last California grizz bit the dust in 1922 (so much for our state animal). Then came the famous Alder Creek gunfight, where farmers forted up and fought off the timber company's gunfighters, who turned out to be recent graduates of San Quentin Peniten-tiary. After a few drunken incidents, the gunfighters wound up on a schooner bound for San Francisco, and the farmers sold out their virgin redwoods to the lumber company for peanuts. So it goes.

Pause at Alder Creek and consider the San Andreas fault. This is where the fault comes ashore and heads down through Southern California. This area took a huge hit in the 1906 earthquake. Much of Point Arena was destroyed; fences were moved six feet—rock-and-roll time for the locals. Remember, this is why Native Americans in this region lived in temporary shelters not unlike a Kelty tent—so they could survive the big ones.

Another good hike is out to the beach and south to the mouth of the Garcia. The Manchester State Beach is a catch basin for sea debris, which accounts for the tremendous amount of driftwood found here. In fact, the beach often looks like a graveyard for driftwood. This is all good for building shelters from the howling north wind. Pass Brush Creek and pretty soon you come to a big lagoon and the Garcia River. Look for many of the same bird species you saw up at Alder Creek. However, the Garcia is steelhead country. You want to be here at high tide in January or February—there's a prime spot called Miner Hole not far from the parking area on Miner Hole Road. Most of the fishermen I've seen here wear waders and work their way downstream. Look for where the locals are fishing and follow their lead.

It's not that Manchester Beach is so cold—the swans think it's tropical—but we humanoids don't have the down feathers. We need good warm clothes because a windchill factor can make 50° feel like freezing. Bring gloves—warm hands make you feel warm. Bring a sweatshirt with a hood for hanging around and sleeping in—most of your heat escapes from your head. Bring earplugs for sleeping—the flapping of the tent might keep you awake.

KEY INFORMATION

Manchester State Beach
P.O. Box 440
Mendocino, CA 95460

Operated by: California Department of Parks and Recreation

Information: (707) 882-2463; http://parks.ca.gov

Open: All year

Individual sites: 46 sites for tents or RVs, 10 environmental sites in the dunes (1-mile level walk from parking lot)

Each site has: Picnic table, fireplace, wood for sale

Registration: By entrance; reserve by phone, (800) 444-7275, or online, www.reserveamerica.com

Facilities: Water, vault toilets

Parking: At individual site

Fee: $7; $8.65 nonrefundable reservation fee

Elevation: Sea level

Restrictions:

Pets—On leash only

Fires—In fireplace

Vehicles—RVs up to 30 feet, trailers up to 22 feet

Other—Reservations on holidays and good weather weekends recommended

To get there: from Point Arena, drive 2 miles north on Highway 1 past Manchester and Home Sweet Home Ranch to Kinney Road. Turn left, and drive to the campground.

MARY SMITH CAMPGROUND

Shasta–Trinity National Forest, near Lewiston

Mary Smith Campground has to be the cutest little tent-only campground in Northern California. The campground is on Lewiston Lake, one of the prettiest lakes for miles around. You can see the snow-covered Trinity Alps. The hills around are forest green. The campsites are cute and cleverly placed to give everyone a lake view. There are flush toilets. There is an affable campground host. Everything is picture perfect. Even the motorboats are under control—a 10-mph speed limit means you won't be run down in your canoe. The cold and clear lake has huge fish. Picturesque Lewiston and Weaverville are nearby, as is great hiking in the Trinity Alps. What's wrong? Nothing's wrong, unless you hate camping below a dam. Still, make an exception for Mary Smith Campground or you'll miss out on an easy-to-access, sublime-to-be-in spot.

Why is the campground named after Mary Smith? Mary Smith was an attractive brunette who was the major stockholder of a dredging company in Lewiston a century-plus ago. She was the only woman to operate a dredge, and she waxed rich at it. The hydraulic and dredge mining in Trinity County (the last county in California to allow this destructive means of mining gold) left the piles of boulders by all the streams.

The dam you see at the head of Lewiston Lake is the Trinity Lake dam. Trinity Lake,

CAMPGROUND RATINGS

Beauty:	★★★★★
Site privacy:	★★★★
Site spaciousness:	★★★★
Quiet:	★★★★
Security:	★★★★★
Cleanliness/upkeep:	★★★★

Mary Smith Campground is a little oasis on Lewiston Lake, a gem surrounded by water-skiing megareservoir lakes. And cultural outings abound nearby

a.k.a. Clair Engle Lake for the senator responsible for the dam (reviled by locals), is a huge reservoir with 150 miles of shoreline—water-ski country. Pacific Gas & Electric is always drawing down the lake, so its shoreline looks like an old bathtub with grime rings. Trinity Lake deserves to be reviled. Still, when the huge Trinity Lake hydroelectric dam is running—pushing water in Lewiston Lake below—run get your fishing rod because the fishing is just fantastic. Anchor out in the current.

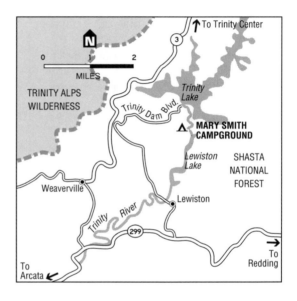

Use worms tossed into the current or drop them down to the bottom. Watch out! An old fisherman at the campground was raving about the size of the fish he caught—brown trout and rainbows—when the plant was pumping water. When it stops, the fishing slows up.

So Lewiston Lake is an afterbay reservoir for Trinity Lake—as a consequence, Lewiston Lake never gets pulled down. It's always cold (Lewiston Lake gets the cooler, lower depths of Trinity Lake) and always beautiful. Unhappily, there is no hiking around Lewiston Lake. Best to head down to Lewiston itself to see the sights.

Take a look at the Trinity River Fish Hatchery below the Lewiston Dam—this is where they make steelhead and trout on the assembly line. Then head down to the Lewiston Hotel for soup and salad (pretty good dinner steaks as well), or try Mama's Place for one of those all-in-one, grease-me-up breakfasts that leave you ready to climb a mountain right away or sign up for a coronary bypass.

A little farther on is Weaverville. This fascinating mining town was more than half Chinese in the 1850s. Chinese? The Chinese were all over this area during the gold mining era. Visit the Weaverville State Historical Park and see for yourself how successful these Chinese were—and how badly they got hosed over by the locals. If possible, visit the Joss House in the park, which is the oldest Chinese temple in continuous use in California. The temple is Taoist, a faith aimed at serenity through harmony with nature—achieved by eliminating ambition to attain purity and simplicity. It's ironic because all the miners, American and Chinese, just tore this county apart looking for gold.

Next door is the J. J. Jackson Museum, with relics and photos of the hydraulic mining, which, along with dredging, was responsible for most of the damage. There is also a fine display of Native American baskets. Consider the baskets and then the hydraulic nozzles.

Never mind. Go eat in the Mexican restaurant next door. The place is run by women, which I find reassuring. And the cook was drinking Mexican beer while she made the food. That's even more reassuring. Don't ask for the food to be hot unless you want it HOT. Homemade, terrific food. The outdoor patio is lovely.

To work it off, take a killer hike (14 miles round-trip). Get in your car and head up Highway 3. At the south end of Trinity Lake, 3 miles south of the Stuart Fork Bridge, go left up a good dirt road to the Rush Creek Lakes Trailhead. This is a major hike (one the rangers call difficult), but it'll clean out your pipes. The trail heads up through the woods for 2 miles, and then you see Monument Peak. Keep climbing (at one point you can see Mount Shasta) to the top of a manzanita-covered knob and ridgeline, and pretty soon you'll see Rush Creek Lakes about 800 feet down.

KEY INFORMATION

Mary Smith Campground, Shasta–Trinity National Forests

Forest Supervisor
2400 Washington Avenue
Redding, CA 96001

Operated by: U.S. Forest Service

Information: (530) 623-2121, (530) 242-2360; www.rs.fs.fed.us/ shastatrinity

Open: May through October (phone ahead to confirm)

Individual sites: 17 sites for tents

Each site has: Picnic table, fireplace

Registration: By entrance

Facilities: Water, flush and vault toilets

Parking: Near individual site

Fee: $9

Elevation: 2,000 feet

Restrictions:

Pets—On leash only

Fires—In fireplace

Vehicles—No RVs or trailers

Other—Check weather conditions and water availabilty

To get there: from Lewiston, drive 2.5 miles north on County Road 105 (Trinity Dam Boulevard) to the campground on the right.

MILL CREEK CAMPGROUND

Del Norte Coast State Park, near Crescent City

Mill Creek Campground is a pretty forest campground in a shaded stream canyon. Take away the redwoods, and this feels like eastern forest. With all the maples, it could be Pennsylvania. Miles off Highway 101, Mill Creek is quiet. The private campsites are backed off in their own little corners. In the summer, when everybody is on the road camping, Mill Creek fills up slowly. It is close to the Klamath River for river adventure. Crescent City is available for an emergency junk food run—or to buy fresh fish fillets to fry back at camp. Prairie Creek Redwoods State Park is just south for trips to see the elk, or you can spend days on Gold Bluffs Beach, the most beautiful undeveloped stretch of sandy beach in California.

Del Norte Coast Redwoods State Park is huge—with 6,400 acres of redwoods, rhododendrons, wildflowers, tidepools, meadows, and beaches. This little corner of California is frontier. Lovely little Trinidad to the south is the last port of call for New Age California. Up here men can fix the truck, catch salmon, rig a crab trap, and run a chain saw. All the women call you "Honey" and sound like they mean it. Fuel for the bellies of the folks in Del Norte County (forget the *e* on Norte) is coffee, beer, and salmon jerky.

Come prepared for wet weather. Think big tent. Big tents are better if you're cooped up for a while. You get less claustrophobic

CAMPGROUND RATINGS

Beauty:	★★★★★
Site privacy:	★★★★★
Site spaciousness:	★★★★
Quiet:	★★★
Security:	★★★★★
Cleanliness/upkeep:	★★★★★

Mill Creek Campground feels like eastern forest camping— this is the last beautiful state park around to fill up on summer weekends.

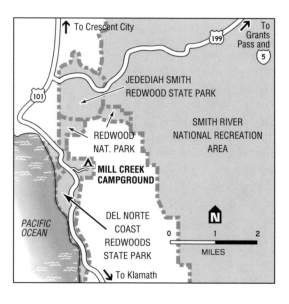

and they're easier to cook in if need be. Also consider a screen house—the mosquitoes can get pesky up here as well. Plus, on a dry night screen houses are fun to sleep in.

Mill Creek Campground is lumberjack country. Hobbs, Wall & Company once set up a private railroad called Del Norte Southern to take the logs out of Mill Creek. The redwoods grow on such steep slopes that the timber company had to build a system of railed "inclines" to the canyon and railroad below. Logs were hauled along the ridges above to an incline, where they were lowered to the canyon and railcars below.

The men did the rest of the work. They chopped the trees, limbed them, and ran the chains. It was brutal, and gave rise to another industry—feeding 165 hungry lumberjacks down in Mill Creek three meals a day. It was serious business—each man had his seat at the table and no one could speak until the meal was over. Mammoth quantities of meat, potatoes, canned vegetables, bread, butter, and dessert were consumed. Talk about carb and protein loading—these boys worked 12 hours a day, ate, and slept. Look at an old photo of the jacks—not a tubby one in the bunch—thin as rails and strong as oxen. On Saturday night they left for the bars and cathouses of Crescent City, returning to Mill Creek Canyon on Monday morning to work. There were kids in the canyon, too, and a lady schoolteacher to educate them. She lived in a log cabin with a drafty roof and rode the incline down to the camp to teach every day.

Hike the Trestle Trail loop along the bed of the old Hobbs, Wall & Company logging railroad that ran beside Mill Creek. Find the trailhead just northeast of the bridge between Cascara (campsites 73 through 125) and Red Alder Campground (campsites 1 through 72). The trail heads up the hillside past big stumps and maples (the alders and maples show rich color in the fall). Cross a wooden bridge and walk along the old railbed. See how the second-growth redwoods have circled the stumps of the trees cut by the company. Half a mile down the railbed, past another bridge, look for what's left of the trestle. Stay on the trail, bearing right until you come down into Red Alder Loop by campsite 7. The whole trip is a little more than a mile.

Other trails out of Mill Creek are the Hobbs Wall Trail, the Mill Creek Trail, the Alder Basin Trail, and the Saddler Skyline Trail. Hike the Damnation Creek Trail down to the little beach with the sea stacks and tidepools. A shorter tidepool walk is the Enderts Beach Trail at the end of Enderts Beach Road. Find the road just south of Crescent City where Humboldt Road goes north. Drive out to Requa (once a Yurok village), and hike north from the end of the road.

Crescent City is the closest supply source. Check out the Del Norte County Historical Society Museum (phone (707) 464-3922 for hours), or the Battery Point Lighthouse. No stranger to mishap, Crescent City was hit by a tsunami, caused by the Alaskan earthquake in 1964, that killed 14 and destroyed the downtown. And a few miles offshore the steamer *Brother Jonathan* hit a reef and 200 passengers drowned. Win some, lose some. This is a big-shouldered frontier town.

To get there: from Crescent City, drive 9 miles south on Highway 101. The entrance to Mill Creek Campground is on the left. Be careful because this is on a blind curve. The campground is several miles east of Highway 101 on the access road.

KEY INFORMATION

Mill Creek Campground
Del Norte Coast Redwoods State Park
1375 Elk Valley Road
Crescent City, CA 95531

Operated by: California Department of Parks and Recreation

Information: (707) 464-6101 ext 5120; http://parks.ca.gov

Open: April through October (phone to confirm)

Individual sites: 145 sites for tents or RVs

Each site has: Picnic table, fireplace

Registration: By entrance; obtain the required permit at Redwood Information Center; reserve by phone, (800) 444-7275, or online, www.reserveusa.com

Facilities: Water, flush toilets, showers, wood for sale

Parking: At individual site

Fee: $12; $8.65 nonrefundable reservation fee

Elevation: 670 feet

Restrictions:

Pets—On leash only

Fires—In fireplace

Vehicles—RVs up to 31 feet, trailers up to 27 feet

Other—15-day stay limit in peak season, 30-day limit in off season; reservations on summer holidays recommended

THE COAST

NADELOS CAMPGROUD / WAILAKI CAMPGROUND

King Range National Conservation Area, near Garberville

These pretty little brother and sister campgrounds are right in the belly of the beast of the Lost Coast, where a fist of mountains rises straight out of the surf and black-sand beach. The terrain is so rugged that highway engineers had to route Highway 1 many miles inland, leaving this huge hunk of land virtually untouched and begging to be explored. Nadelos or Wailaki campground makes a perfect base to do exactly that.

On top of each other, Nadelos and Wailaki are virtually the same campground. Coming off Shelter Cove Road, Nadelos is first—the eight campsites are a short walk from the parking lot and are tucked into a hill across little Bear Creek. Half a mile south is the entrance to Wailaki, which is engineered for trailers and RVs but wonderful for tent camping as well. Last time I was there—in the fall of 1996—both campgrounds were vacant, so we stayed at Wailaki, in one of the larger campsites. Both campgrounds have water and were recently reengineered, so the sites look clean and inviting, and the new-style pit toilets are immaculate.

The valley is oriented north to south, so don't expect much sunlight at either Nadelos or Wailaki, except in the middle of the day. In fact, don't expect much sunlight on the Lost Coast unless you come in September or October, the region's premium weather months.

CAMPGROUND RATINGS

Beauty:	★★★★★
Site privacy:	★★★★★
Site spaciousness:	★★★★★
Quiet:	★★★★
Security:	★★
Cleanliness/upkeep:	★★★★★

Nadelos and Wailaki Campgrounds make a good base camp for exploring the fabulous Lost Coast. Try to come in September and October to get the beautiful weather.

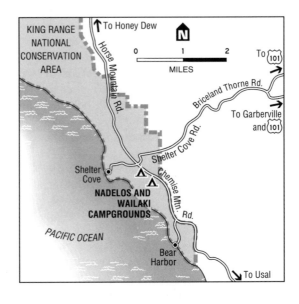

KING RANGE NATIONAL CONSERVATION AREA

↑ To Honey Dew

N

0   1   2
MILES

To 101

Briceland Thorne Rd.

To Garberville and 101

Horse Mountain Rd.

Shelter Cove Rd.

Chemise Mtn. Rd.

Shelter Cove

NADELOS AND WAILAKI CAMPGROUNDS

PACIFIC OCEAN

Bear Harbor

↘ To Usal

From October through April, the Lost Coast is one of the wettest spots on the Pacific Coast. In wet years, the Lost Coast can get up to 200 inches of rain. That's 16 feet! April and May are often windy, and the landscape is at its most lush. In June, July, and August sunshine alternates with thick fog. Ah, but September and October are heaven. The hills are golden, and the sunsets explode across the sky.

Of course, tucked into the woods at Nadelos or Waila-ki, don't expect to see the sunset. You have to drive down to the beach at Shelter Cove to see that. Shelter Cove used to be a giant sheep ranch but now has been developed into a real estate nightmare. Retirees come in, build huge houses, go crazy from the isolation of the Lost Coast, and run screaming back to civilization. So there are lots of big houses going for very few dollars at Shelter Cove.

But there are wonderful beaches as well. Black Sands Beach at the north end of town basically continues 24 miles north to the mouth of the Mattole River. This is a famous hike that folks usually take from north to south because of the prevailing winds. Hikers should bring water (or a water-purifying device), a tidal schedule to time certain beaches, and camping equipment. In town, near the Pelican Landings Restaurant, find the short trail to Little Black Sands Beach, which is a favorite of the locals. And, of course, south of town past the Shelter Cove Marina and Campground is Dead Man's Beach—famous among beach people.

While you are in town, don't miss the fish and chips at the Shelter Cove Campground Deli. The fish is incredible—caught fresh every morning. The chips are thick and light. The portions are enormous. I asked for a half portion, and the tiny woman at the counter laughed. "If I can eat a whole order, so can you, big boy!" she said, and she was right. I sat outside at the picnic tables with my fish and chips and beer, with the sun setting on the whole Pacific Ocean before me.

At both Nadelos and Wailaki campground, you'll spot signed trails that head west to both the Lost Coast Trail and the Hidden Valley Trail. The Hidden Valley Trail heads north 1.75 miles to the Chemise Mountain Road, where you can walk back south past the little cabins to the campgrounds. The trail south goes to Chemise Mountain (3 miles round-trip) and Whale Gulch (10 miles round-trip). Look for a herd of transplanted Roosevelt elk along the way.

Bring water. The nearest water on the Whale Gulch trail is at the Needle Rock Visitor Center 6 miles away. It's not a bad idea to stash a car or arrange a pick-up at the Visitor Center for the trip back. (To reach Needle Rock from the campgrounds, head south on Chemise Mountain Road to Four Corners, then go right on Briceland Road to Needle Rock.)

For a grueling but fun road trip, turn south on Usal Road at Four Corners and drive down to Usal Beach and Highway 1. Phone the Sinkyone Wilderness State Park at (707) 986-7711 to get a reading on the road conditions. Impassable in winter, this road hasn't changed much since Jack London and his wife, Charmian, came up in a wagon in 1911.

To get there: from Redway (by Garberville) on Highway 101, drive 22 miles west on Shelter Cove Road. Go 2 miles south on Chemise Mountain Road to Nadelos Campground, then another 0.5 miles south to Wailaki Campground.

KEY INFORMATION

Nadelos or Wailaki Campground
Arcata Resource Area, U.S. Bureau of Land Management
1695 Heindon Road
Arcata, CA 95521

Operated by: U.S. Department of the Interior, Bureau of Land Management

Information: (707) 825-2300; www.ca.blm.gov/arcata

Open: All year (depending on road and weather conditions)

Individual sites: Nadelos has 8 tent-only sites; Wailaki has 13 sites for tents or RVs

Each site has: Picnic table, fire ring

Registration: At entrance

Facilities: Water, pit toilets

Parking: At individual site

Fee: $8

Elevation: 1,840 feet

Restrictions:

Pets—On leash only

Fires—In fire ring

Vehicles—RVs and trailers at Wailaki only (no hookups)

Other—14-day stay limit; don't leave food out

THE COAST

COAST

OAK BOTTOM ON THE SALMON RIVER CAMPGROUND

Klamath National Forest, near Somes Bar

Oak Bottom on the Salmon River Campground is perfect for those summer days when it's hotter than hell, even at a 700-foot elevation where the Salmon River meets the Klamath. You've been rafting out in the sun all day; you want a beer; and you want to crash in your tent where it's cool and dark and, maybe, saw enormous piles of wood in your sleep. You want to wake up the next day ready for more wonderful adventures on the insanely beautiful rivers. Oak Bottom is where you want to go. The campground is cool and dark under heavily canopied trees—perfect for August dog days (Native Americans thought so, too). The sites are perfect for tent camping. Most of the picnic tables and tent pitches are 10 yards away from the parking spot. The sites are well separated, and the predominant feeling here at Oak Bottom is friendliness. Somes Bar is next door for ice, beer, soda, and hot dogs (or head up to the markets at Orleans—one has a pretty good meat counter).

Right across unbusy Salmon River Road is the Salmon River—famous in these parts for being the clearest, most unspoiled river in the area. In fact, last time I was at Oak Bottom the river was magnificently clear, but Fish and Game wouldn't allow fishing because people were catching too many steelhead. It wasn't fair.

Out by the river, in the afternoon, we could see the flash of the fish as they

CAMPGROUND RATINGS

Beauty:	★★★★★
Site privacy:	★★★★★
Site spaciousness:	★★★★★
Quiet:	★★★★
Security:	★★★★★
Cleanliness/upkeep:	★★★★

Open all year, Oak Bottom on the Salmon River is a great base camp for fishing, rafting, hiking, and bicycling by the Salmon and Klamath Rivers.

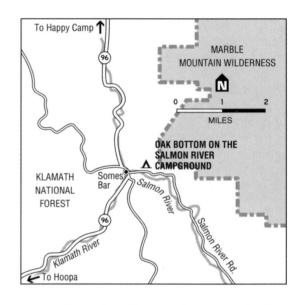

To Happy Camp →

96

MARBLE
MOUNTAIN WILDERNESS

N

0   1   2

MILES

OAK BOTTOM ON THE
SALMON RIVER
CAMPGROUND

KLAMATH
NATIONAL
FOREST

Somes
Bar

Salmon River

96

Klamath River

Salmon River Rd.

← To Hoopa

headed upstream. Steelhead want to spawn just like the salmon. The female steelhead digs the nest, and as she lays her eggs, her mate fertilizes them. She digs another nest a foot or so upstream and uses the gravel to cover the first. Her mate fertilizes the second nest. This procedure continues until the female is out of eggs and her dutiful mate is exhausted.

Their young hatch and swim out of the gravel. After a year or two (up to four years for slow developers), the young steelhead head out to sea, where they'll eat and grow up before returning to spawn themselves. These beautiful fish once spawned in all the rivers and streams as far south as Baja California. (Even Malibu and Topanga Creeks near Los Angeles had a steelhead run in recent memory.)

Unfortunately, dams, water diversions, logging, overgrazing by cattle, and pollution have pushed the steelhead spawn farther and farther north. Fortunately, steelhead are a very resilient fish. Improve the habitat and they'll come back.

Next time I come to Oak Bottom, I'll bring a bicycle. The Salmon River Road up to Forks of Salmon is a one-lane road, twisting up by the wild gorge of the glass-clear Salmon River. Drive the road in a car, and you are constantly terrified a logging truck coming the other way will take you out. So you drive with your lights on and window rolled down to listen, blow your horn at every curve (there are thousands), and pray to the Virgin Mary for the best. On a bike, you could hear a logging truck miles away and have tons of time to pull over and find a rock niche for yourself and your bike. It's a pretty steady uphill to

Forks of Salmon (from 700 to 1,242 feet), but all the way this ribbon of sublimity, the Salmon River in its white granite canyon, unwinds before you. On a bike, you could check out all the great pools and ways to get down to the river, and then ditch the bike and hike down to them. (There are zero places to park a car on this hairy road.)

On the way, pass Nordheimer Creek Campground. This lovely little campground is fun in the spring when all the flowers are out. By summer, it gets dusty and hot. Somebody told me Nordheimer was like a pizza oven in August. Check out the piles of rocks by the river. There's a dredge site down in the river—this area was mined for gold. There is potable water at Nordheimer in an enclosed storage tank, but I would check with the Ranger Station in Orleans before I counted on finding water there. Ride as far as Forks of Salmon for a soda and hamburger, then coast on back down the hill to Oak Bottom on the Salmon River Campground.

Find good hiking at the Wooley Creek Trailhead 3 miles up Salmon Creek Road from the campground. The first half-mile of the trail is steep and hot. Then you crest at "Golden Elbow," where you can see the Salmon River Canyon, Wooley Creek, and your automobile parked in the lot about 600 feet below. Then the going is easier, and the trail sweeps down along Wooley Creek, crosses pretty Gates Creek, and cuts through rocky Haypress Creek gorge to Wooley Camp. At this point, about 6 miles into the hike, it should be time to eat some lunch and think about heading back down to Oak Bottom on the Salmon River for late afternoon fishing, drinks, and dinner.

KEY INFORMATION

Oak Bottom on the Salmon River Campground, Klamath National Forest

Ukonom Ranger District

P.O. Drawer 410

Orleans, Ca 95556-0410

Operated by: U.S. Forest Service

Information: (530) 627-32911, (530) 842-6131; www.r5.fs.fed.us/klamath

Open: April–November 5

Individual sites: 26 sites for tents and small RVs

Each site has: Picnic table, fireplace

Registration: By entrance

Facilities: Water, vault toilets

Parking: At individual site

Fee: $10

Elevation: 700 feet

Restrictions:

Pets—On leash only

Fires—In fireplace

Vehicles—Suitable for small RVs only

Other—Check weather conditions and water availabilty

To get there, turn east onto the Salmon River Road at Somes Bar, and drive 3 miles to the campground.

COAST

PATRICK'S POINT STATE PARK

near Trinidad

Most beautiful of all California's state parks, Patrick's Point is full of enchanted Sitka spruce groves and dizzying cliffs running down to ancient sea stacks, sea lions, and the foaming green Pacific. The three campground loops in the park, Agate, Penn, and Abalone, are under trees—the campsites nestled in bracken fern, sword fern, and salmonberry. The Sitkas, with their silver moss, crinkled bark, and golden cones, loom out of the mist. Each site is private, secluded, and special. On the beach, find agates and sometimes jade. Surf fish for perch and flounder. With the Yurok village of Sumeg in the park, and Trinidad nearby with the marine lab and party fishing boats, there's lots to do with kids.

Take the Rim Trail to get a sense of the headlands. Accessible from various places, the trail goes 2 miles around the promontory, passing little trails to Palmers Point, Abalone Point, Rocky Point, Patrick's Point, Wedding Rock, and Mussel Rocks. By the time you take all these spur trails, the trip is more like 4 miles. Wedding Rock is a good place to look for whales during the season.

Head to Palmer's Point and climb down to the tidepool area. Look for sea lions and harbor seals. The sea lions are bigger than the seals, without spots, and their buff-to-brown hide looks black when it is wet. Sea lions are the fastest swimmers—up to 25 mph when pressed. They can descend to

CAMPGROUND RATINGS

Beauty:	★★★★★
Site privacy:	★★★★★
Site spaciousness:	★★★★
Quiet:	★★★
Security:	★★★★★
Cleanliness/upkeep:	★★★★★

Patrick's Point Campground has everything—beauty, sea lions, a Native American village, and hot clam chowder nearby.

450 feet and stay submerged for 20 minutes. They use sonar to get around and find prey.

Hike down to Agate Beach where the agate finding is easiest after a high tide. Best hunting, though, is after a winter storm. The agates found here are unpolished and look just like little white and bluish quartz stones. Take them home and put them in a bottle with oil so they always look wet and pretty. Keep hiking for 2 miles and come to Humboldt Lagoons State Park.

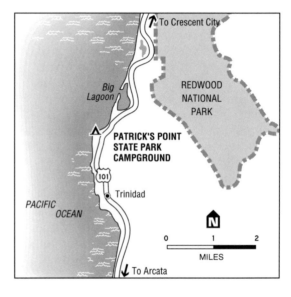

These lagoons are the sand-drowned mouths of streams. Spits of wave-borne sand form across their outlets to dam up the streams until the ocean cuts a floodgate through. Check out the dunes for beach pea, salt grass, verbena, and sea rocket. On the shore is more Sitka spruce, red alder, and redwood. This was prime Yurok Native American country.

The Yuroks moved between fishing and hunting camps. They trapped elk in deep pits covered with branches and dirt, and they speared sea lions by painting their own bodies dark and wriggling up close enough for the kill. They netted ducks and geese and gill-netted salmon. The women gathered acorns and leached them, and made bread. Dried eel was a specialty (a big hit with hungry European explorers). Abalone was an everyday staple, as well as edible seaweed. The Yuroks lived well.

At the foot of the lagoons is Big Lagoon County Park, with a boat ramp for canoers, kayakers, and Windsurfers. Consider the tent camping here for another trip or if Patrick's Point is jammed up. You are at water ground zero just off the Big Lagoon. The tent pitches are grassy sand. There's good camping (no reservations), but not much of the cover privacy that Patrick's Point has in spades. I talked to the ranger there who said the fishing is pretty slim until the ocean cuts through the dunes. Then you get steelhead, sea-run cutthroat trout, sharks, flounders, and so on. To drive to Big Lagoon County Park from Patrick's Point, just go 1 mile north on Highway 101. Turn left at Big Lagoon Road, and follow the signs.

Another good trip is to nearby Trinidad. Everyone likes the Humboldt State lab and aquarium (open weekdays 9:00 A.M to 5:00 P.M.). Sir Francis Drake once anchored at this old whaling town, which now offers peerless clam chowder and crab sandwiches at the Seascape Restaurant down on the Trinidad Wharf. The fish and crab come off the fishing boats and directly through the kitchen door of Seascape.

Come here in July and go for salmon. There are charter and party boats available, and the fish are sometimes close enough for small boats. A word of warning though: This coast is notorious for fogging in, so watch your navigation or you'll end up in Hawaii.

No luck fishing? Stop at Katy's Smokehouse on Edwards Street across from the Trinidad Memorial Lighthouse to buy fish or crab to take back to camp. When the Dungeness come in November, Katy's is crab-lovers' heaven, and her smoked albacore is incomparable.

The Yuroks revered Patrick's Point and believed that the spirit of the porpoises lived here and that the seven sea stacks were the last earthly abode of the immortals. Patrick Beegan, an Irishman who came here in 1851, just liked the wild Indian potatoes (lily bulbs) that grew here. Hence Patrick's Point.

KEY INFORMATION

Patrick's Point State Park
4150 Patrick's Point Drive
Trinidad, CA 95570

Operated by: California Department of Parks and Recreation

Information: (707) 677-3570; http://parks.ca.gov

Open: All year

Individual sites: 124 (only Agate Beach) sites for tents or RVs

Each site has: Picnic table, fireplace

Registration: By entrance; reserve by phone, (800) 444-7275, or online, www.reserveamerica.com

Facilities: Water, flush toilets, showers, wood for sale

Parking: At individual site

Fee: $12; $8.65 nonrefundable reservation fee

Elevation: 100 feet

Restrictions:

Pets—On leash only; $1 fee

Fires—In fireplace

Vehicles—RVs up to 31 feet

Other—Reservations on holidays and summer weekends required

To get there: from Trinidad, go 5 miles north on Highway 101 to the Patrick's Point State Park entrance on the left.

COAST

RUSSIAN GULCH STATE PARK
Mendocino

Thank God for F.D.R. and the New Deal, or we wouldn't have Russian Gulch State Park and the soaring arched concrete bridge that spans the gulch. What a pretty little campground! Take a left just after the bridge and circle down a curved one-lane access road, to the campground in the canyon and the beach across the stream under the bridge. The beach is all white sandbars, narrow blue water, soaring black cliffs spotted white, and green headlands. Protected, there is safe swimming here and an easy launch for kayaks or inflatables.

The campground threads its way up the ferned canyon, with sites on either side of the access road. Cozy, mossy, and primal—that's what you feel tucked into a tent under the giant ferns, alders, redwoods, and hemlocks. Come here to sun on a safe beach. Fish for rockfish. Hike the Fern Canyon Trail. Hike the South Trail to Mendocino, where you can eat world-class food; shop till you drop; and hang with the rich, famous, and alternative.

Who named Russian Gulch? Nobody remembers, but local folks think the Russian fur hunters used to store bales of furs here in the otter- and seal-slaughtering days of the early 1800s. The Russkies operated out of Fort Ross down the coast and used Eskimo hunters in *baidarkas* (sealskin kayaks) to do the stalking and killing. The local Pomo Indians, who knew something about the sea and the seals themselves

CAMPGROUND RATINGS

Beauty:	★★★★★
Site privacy:	★
Site spaciousness:	★★
Quiet:	★★
Security:	★★★★
Cleanliness/upkeep:	★★★★

Russian Gulch State Park Campground sits beside an azure gem of a cove next to the "jewel of the north coast," the town of Mendocino.

(stalking them by painting themselves dark and pretending to be seals to get close enough for a kill), were amazed by the Eskimos' skill in using their kayaks for the hunt. However, after the seals were mostly dead, the Russkies packed up and headed for home, leaving the Mendocino coast and the surviving Pomos easy pickings for a motley crew of honky forty-niners who followed the wreck of the *Frolic*.

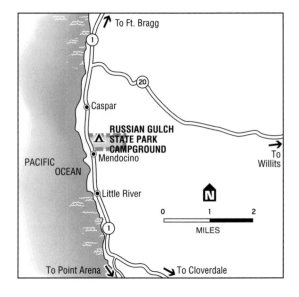

The two-masted clipper ship named *Frolic* sank off Russian Gulch in 1850 with a hull full of Chinese silks and gewgaws. Henry Meigs sent his boys from San Francisco to salvage the wreck, but they found only happy Pomo Native American women wearing skirts of Chinese silk and jewelry fashioned from oriental beads. Inevitably, Meigs heard about the huge redwoods in these parts and immediately sent a steam sawmill up to Mendocino to start ripping boards to build San Francisco, shore up gold mines in the Sierra Nevada, and make railroad ties for the Transcontinental Railway. The place boomed, with dozens of bars and hotels to entertain the hard-partying lumberjacks.

After that, Mendocino boomed and busted and finally emerged around 1960 as the "jewel of the north coast"—a pretty little town full of arts, culture, great grub, scenic splendor, and a potpourri of Victorian gothics, New England saltboxes, and false-front Western houses. I love Mendocino. People rag on it for being too cutsie, but I love it just the way it is—perfect for a couple of days of hanging out. The campground is an easy walk from town—just head up the South Trail where it leaves the beach road opposite the group camp.

You come up over the bluffs, then walk along Highway 1 before taking the first right toward Mendocino.

Back at camp, hike the Fern Canyon Trail. This is a 6-mile round-trip trail that allows cyclists as far as the start of the Waterfall Loop. Head east through the campground. Look for nettles, salmonberry, and nightshade down by the creek, and alder, hazel, and laurel by the trail. After half a mile, you begin to see redwoods. At 1.5 miles there are some picnic tables. Beyond here, no bicycles are allowed. Hike up to the falls and admire. Then take the loop around to the right, back to the picnic tables, and retrace the trail back to the campground.

Another good walk is the Headland Trail. This 1-mile trail circles the park's north headland, showing off the incredible surf-carved rocks and cliffs. At the southwest end, look for a blowhole fed by a sea cave. Big waves blast up through the blowhole. Inland, look for the punch bowl where the roof of another cave collapsed. Plants hang over the rim, but the sea comes in through a small opening and washes the floor clean.

Good fun is canoeing the Big River. Phone Catch-a-Canoe & Bicycles, Too! at (707) 937-0273 to rent watercraft and see seals, ducks, ospreys, and other wild critters. The Big River is an estuary, which means tidal, so you want to go upriver when the tide is coming in and downriver when the tide is going out. Go back to the jolly folks at Catch-a-Canoe and rent bicycles for a run up Little Lake Road to Caspar Orchard Road and back.

While camping at Russian Gulch, shop at Mendosa's and buy cheese at the deli kitty-cornered from Mendosa's. Don't forget to grab a burger at Meno Burgers, nearby on Lansing Street (the veggie burger is heartily recommended).

KEY INFORMATION

Russian Gulch State Park
P.O. Box 440
Mendocino, CA 95460

Operated by: California Department of Parks and Recreation

Information: (707) 937-5804; http://parks.ca.gov

Open: April 1 through November 1

Individual sites: 28 sites for tents or RVs

Each site has: Picnic table, fireplace

Registration: By entrance; reserve by phone, (800) 444-7275, or online www.reserveamerica.com

Facilities: Water, flush toilets, showers, wood for sale

Parking: At individual site

Fee: $12—May 1 through September 30; $8.65 nonrefundable reservation fee

Elevation: 100 feet

Restrictions:

Pets—On leash only

Fires—In fireplace

Vehicles—RVs up to 27 feet, trailers up to 24 feet

Other—Permit required; 8 people per site; reservations in summer recommended

To get there: from Mendocino, go 2 miles north on Highway 1 to the campground entrance on the left.

TREE OF HEAVEN CAMPGROUND

Klamath National Forest, near Yreka

The Tree of Heaven Campground comes as a stunning surprise. One moment you are driving along the Klamath in high sage country. You pass an old-time girder bridge (Ash Creek Bridge), sweep around a curve, and see the Forest Service sign to the Tree of Heaven Campground. The entry drive drops suddenly down to the river, and there you are at the Tree of Heaven Campground, and you suddenly feel like you've been invited to an English garden party. All over there's green tended grass. The campsites are on grass. There's room for baseball and, in the day use area, horseshoes, an open-pit BBQ, and a volley-ball court with a net in tournament shape. Everything is neat and pruned. The wood-for-sale pile by the host trailer is squared away. The campers look well groomed. Even the campers' lap dogs are well maintained and strut around Tree of Heaven on their leads like little British marines.

The Klamath rolls by the campground like a watery muscle. Most campers swim right in front of the camp off the boat launch. Here the river runs pretty slowly, but everybody keeps a close eye on any kids, pets, or poor swimmers because this water is headed for the Pacific Ocean. Fishing can be great. One ranger I talked to said he was catching fish right and left up at Tree of Heaven in late September. Last time I was through there, I was told the fish were running but nobody was catch-

CAMPGROUND RATINGS

Beauty:	★★★★★
Site privacy:	★★★★
Site spaciousness:	★★★★★
Quiet:	★★★★★
Security:	★★★★★
Cleanliness/upkeep:	★★★★★

Like an English garden, Tree of Heaven Campground is good for lawn sports, river rafting, fishing, and touristing at nearby Yreka.

ing anything yet. A lady ranger said the salmon were pretty beat up by the time they get that far, but her kids always catch good-eating steelhead trout.

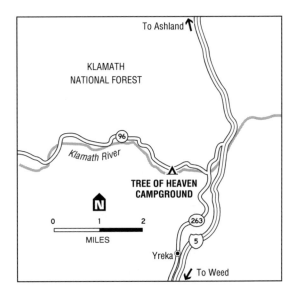

There are hikes around Tree of Heaven—including an interpretive hike near the day use area. Take the Tree of Heaven Trail that heads down by the river about 2 miles. It takes you to a good fishing place. But to really step out, you need to get in your car and head back toward I-5. Turn right on Ash Creek Bridge, which you passed on the way in. A mostly dirt road runs west down the south side of the Klamath. This is good hiking (as long as your dogs last) and great mountain biking. The road winds around with the river until it hits Walker Bridge about 25 miles downstream. On the way, you'll pass Humbug Creek Road, which is worth a look, assuming you're on your mountain bike and don't mind a climb, of course. By Walker Bridge on Highway 96 is the Oak Knoll Ranger Station, so you can use the phone, beg for help, try to hitch a ride, or steel yourself for the climb back up to Tree of Heaven Campground.

The name of the game here is rafting. Best to phone the Ranger Station a week or so in advance and get the name of a reputable rafting outfitter and arrange a trip. Locals, of course, know the waters and use their own rafts. I firmly believe that discretion for strangers in these parts is the better part of valor. Spending a little money up front can save you a lot of grief later—especially if you bring your family along. The outfitters have helmets and life vests. Get it right the first time, and then maybe come back the next year with your own stuff.

Yreka (pronounce the Y then say "reka," or be roundly mocked by the locals), is a major draw only 15 minutes away. The trick is not to get on I-5 when going to and from Yreka. Not only is the exit confusing, but you lose all the sense of "being" in Yreka or in Tree of Heaven. Yreka is a wonderful little town founded by Abraham Thompson back in 1851, who watched in amazement as his grazing mules brought up flecks of gold tangled in the roots of the grass. In six weeks 2,000 miners arrived, and soon there were 27 saloons (first things first!). Now, there's a good sports on the corner of Miner and Main Street.

In the Siskiyou County Museum, Yreka has the best small-museum exhibit of Native American life and crafts I've ever seen. Then there's the eye-popping nuggets in the county courthouse, all the incredible Victorian houses (walk, don't drive), the Blue Goose train that steams through the Shasta Valley to Montague and back again (phone (530) 842-4146 for a schedule of the different runs), and all of the very friendly people.

Tired of camping? Spend an inexpensive but very comfortable night in the Wayside Inn. Right next door is a diner that serves up a whopper breakfast for a pinch of gold dust.

The tree that gives the campground its name is a Chinese tree (*Ailanthus altissima*), commonly called the Tree of Heaven. Chinese laborers planted the tree by gold mines and along railroad tracks. Known as a weed tree because it spreads by root suckers and "airplane-propeller" seeds, the Tree of Heaven is attractive and indestructible.

KEY INFORMATION

Tree of Heaven Campground, Klamath National Forest
Scott River Ranger District
11263 N. Highway 3
Fort Jones, CA 96032-9702

Operated by: U.S. Forest Sevice

Information: (530) 468-5351; www.r5/fs.fed.us/klamath

Open: All year; hosted May through October (phone ahead for weather)

Individual sites: 19

Each site has: Picnic table, fireplace

Registration: By entrance; reserve by phone at (530) 468-5331

Facilities: Water, vault toilets

Parking: At individual site

Fee: $10

Elevation: 2,100 feet

Restrictions:

Pets—On leash only

Fires—In fireplace

Vehicles—Small RVs only

Other—Check weather conditions and water availabilty; no OHV use, no livestock allowed

To get there, drive about 10 miles north of Yreka on Highway 263. Turn left (west) on Highway 96. Pass the Ash Creek Bridge. Look for the Tree of Heaven Campground sign a few miles farther on the left. Be careful on the turn. Or drive 10 miles north on I-5 to Highway 96. Exit and go west on Highway 96 to the campground on the left after passing the Ash Creek Bridge.

COAST

VAN DAMME STATE PARK
Little River

V an Damme State Park lies along the most beautiful stretch of coast in America where it doesn't snow during the wintertime (unlike Maine). There is a sandy beach where folks actually dare swim, whales, abalone, antique shops, a pygmy forest, fabulous restaurants, and tent pitches on moss so soft you sleep like a baby. This is a well-run, friendly park. There are rangers, docents, and a campground host. Open all year, Van Damme is a park for all seasons.

Charles Van Damme was a Flemish kid who busted a gut working in a sawmill in Little River after the Civil War. He went on to operate the Richmond–San Rafael ferry but he left his heart in Little River. When he got some bucks, he bought 40 acres there and later willed them to the State of California. That land became the core of Van Damme State Park—now 2,163 acres of beach and upland.

Well before Charles, Native Americans lived along here as far back as 10,000 years. Of course, in those days, the sea level was 250 feet lower than it is today, so the shore where they gathered food was about 2 miles west in the briny deep, and the grassy headlands where we hike today were then pine forest.

Around 1587, a Spaniard on a galleon named this coast Mendocino for his friend back home—Antonio de Mendosa. A couple hundred years later the Russians came

CAMPGROUND RATINGS

Beauty:	★★★★★
Site privacy:	★
Site spaciousness:	★★★★
Quiet:	★
Security:	★★★
Cleanliness/upkeep:	★★★★★

Come for the ocean, the whales, the Pygmy Forest, and nearby Mendocino, where the TV show Murder, She Wrote *was filmed.*

for the sea-otter pelts and were soon followed by the padres and the forty-niners, who were smitten by the beauty of the place and who settled here after driving out the defenseless Pomo Native Americans. When Smeaton Chase, the eccentric English traveler, came through in 1911, he described the area as "such headlands, black and wooded, such purple seas, such vivid blaze of spray, such fiords and islets…" and the town of Little River itself as "a pretty, straggling village

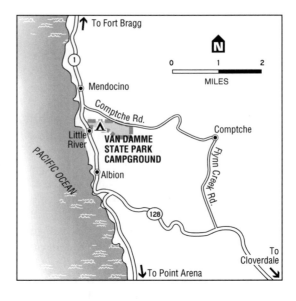

of high gabled houses with quaint dormers and windows, and red roses clambering all about."

Little River is still pretty, and fun. Find the Little River Golf & Tennis Club—open to the public—and food and spirits at the Little River Restaurant and the Little River Inn. Or go a mile or so north to the much-fabled Mendocino, home to many restaurants, shops, and colorful locals. You may recognize it as Cabot Cove, Maine, the hometown of the fictional character Jessica Fletcher of *Murder, She Wrote.*

Watch for whales. Best to look between December and May in the morning when the sea is calm. The gray whales migrate from the Bering Sea to Baja California, where they give birth to their 1,500-pound calves. Mama weighs in at about 30 tons. Look for them blowing water before diving down 100 feet for three or four minutes. To take a closer look at these behemoths, take a whale-watching boat out of Noyo Harbor in Fort Bragg (10 miles to the north).

There's a couple of decent hikes in the park. Head up the Fern Canyon Trail, which starts as a fire road at the east end of Lower Campground. Pass sword fern and redwood, hemlock, and fir along the canyon. By Little River grow alder, salmonberry, and thimbleberry. After 2 miles, the fire road ends (bicycles are allowed this far), and the trail goes deeper into Fern Canyon through Doug fir, redwood, and a plethora of fern. The trail heads out of the canyon and circles back to the right, passing a redwood stump about ten feet in diameter.

When you reach a junction with a dirt road, you can go left to the Pygmy Forest, where old-growth trees have one-inch diameters and heights of four feet! Why? The soil is hard and mineralized, so the cypress and Bolander pine are stunted but produce an impressive crop of pinecones. In between these trees, look for tan oak and rhododendron as well as blackberries and wax myrtle. Just beyond the Pygmy Forest is the Little River Airport Road, which heads back to Little River and Highway 1. You can catch a ride back to camp, or head back through the Pygmy Forest to the trail you hiked in on.

Back at campground central, take a stroll around the Bog Trail loop. This half-mile walk begins near the group camp where the forest meets the wetland. Watch out, the boardwalks are slippery when wet

The two campgrounds, Highland Meadow and Lower, are only a few hundred yards apart. Between the two, I prefer Highland Meadow because it gets you up into the sun. Lower Campground tends to be dark and cool, and gets the bicycle and foot traffic heading up Fern Canyon. Still, in the winter, it is the only campground open.

Be sure to reserve a campsite—especially for summer weekends. This coast is very popular. The beach is across busy Highway 1, so be careful—extra careful if you have children.

Van Damme State Park
P.O. Box 440
Mendocino, CA 94560

Operated by: California Department of Parks and Recreation

Information: (707) 937-5804; http://parks.ca.gov

Open: All year

Individual sites: 74 sites for tents or RVs, 10 hike-in sites in Fern Canyon; also a group site for up to 50 people

Each site has: Picnic table, fireplace

Registration: By entrance; reserve by phone, (800)444-7275, or online, www.resrveamerica.com

Facilities: Water, flush toilets, hot showers, wood for sale

Parking: At individual site

Fee: $12; $8.65 nonrefundable reservation fee

Elevation: 15 feet

Restrictions:

Pets—On leash only

Fires—In fireplace

Vehicles—RVs up to 35 feet

Other—Reservations required from April 1 to October; 2 week stay limit; up to 8 people per site

To get there: from Mendocino, drive 3 miles south on Highway 1 to the Van Damme Park entrance on the left.

NORTHERN CALIFORNIA

THE CASCADES

THE CASCADES

ASPEN CAMPGROUND / MERRIL CAMPGROUND

Eagle Lake, Lassen National Forest, near Susanville

Eagle Lake is so uniquely beautiful that you have to go there, and it is so far from anywhere that you have to stay for a while. Don't bother lugging food supplies all the way to Eagle Lake—buy everything in nearby downtown Susanville, a town so western you expect Wyatt Earp to saunter out of one of the square brick buildings on Main Street in his bowler hat, toting a six-gun. Then you look around and see the supermarket, gas station and bank. All the same, Susanville is a real cowboy town.

There are two ways into Eagle Lake from Susanville. One is up A1 off Highway 44, and the other is up Merrillville Road off Highway 139. Both routes take you through a pass where you'll see Eagle Lake below— the second-largest natural freshwater lake in California (Lake Tahoe is split by a state boundary). All the campgrounds are down on the south end of the lake—all connected by a great new bicycle path that winds its way through the woods and lakeshore. What a beautiful place!

The campgrounds—Aspen, Eagle, Merrill, and Christie—are run by the University Foundation, California State University at Chico, to give students in Recreation and Parks Management some hands-on experience. It really shows. The whole camping experience at Eagle Lake feels clean, intelligent, and supremely enjoyable.

Aspen Campground, for tent camping only, is a pretty little place on a knoll near

CAMPGROUND RATINGS

Beauty:	★★★★★
Site privacy:	★★★★★
Site spaciousness:	★★★★★
Quiet:	★★★★
Security:	★★★★★
Cleanliness/upkeep:	★★★★★

Merrill and Aspen Campgrounds are true destination campgrounds—you have to work to get there and then you'll want to stay for at least a week.

the swimming beach and the marina. There's a store with showers, a laundromat, and bicycles to rent. Eagle Campground is nearby, maybe a quarter of a mile from the marina, but too near the road to suit me. The last time I was at the lake, we camped down at Merrill Campground, which is for RVs and tents together. Merrill became my wife's favorite campground in California. Why? She liked the osprey family ceaselessly swinging over the lake looking for fish. She liked the Canada

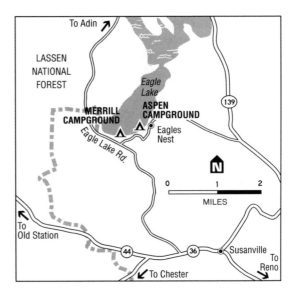

geese and the white pelicans, and she spent hours trying to sight a bald eagle. No luck this time.

I agree with her. Merrill Campground is even better than Aspen Campground. For one thing, I liked being away from the marina. There was less boat and vehicle traffic. The camp sites are all well spaced, and if you want more solitude, you can camp off the beach. If you want lakefront camping, remember to reserve. The best Merrill sites are 166, 168, 170, 172, 174, 176, 178, and 180. The only problem with these sites along the lake is the sun and the light reflected off the water. There is some cover, but bring shade—umbrellas that fit on your beach chair, one of the new shade tents, or a sombrero. Don't forget to bring along buckets of sunscreen to slop on your exposed limbs.

Of course, many sites are first come, first served. You can also camp in a reservable site if you arrive and find it empty. Just check with the reservations host (in a separate trailer from the campground host), who will tell you if the site is open for the day. Best is to arrive, find a site that you would be happy with, park the car, then nose around to see if you can find something better.

Next, get out your fishing rod. The fishing is reputedly great. Although I did not personally wash a worm—and did hear some fishermen grousing—Eagle Lake has a reputation for the famous Eagle Lake rainbow trout. Apparently, the lake water is alkaline, which gives this subspecies of trout an extraordinary flavor.

The Native Americans were always leery of Eagle Lake. Maybe it was the taste of the trout, or maybe it was the earthquake activity around Eagle Lake. But, in any case, they never established permanent camps around the lake. The Maidu and Paiutes would cruise through for a little fishing or hunting but didn't stay long. They believed that a huge Nessie-style serpent lived in the lake. They also believed that Eagle Lake was connected to faraway Pyramid Lake by an underground river. Pyramid Lake is about 100 miles away in Nevada. What gives this legend credence is that contemporary scientists can't seem to account for the apparent interdependent changing water levels in the two lakes.

For the two nights we were in Merrill Campground, we rented a boat (reasonably priced), tossed in sleeping bags and flashlights, and rode north until we found a particularly pristine bit of shoreline on which to sleep. (The pines of the south give way to sagebrush and juniper as you go north.) In the morning, we zipped back to Merrill Campground in time for breakfast.

To get there: from Susanville, go 3 miles west on Highway 36, then 16 miles north on A1 (Eagle Lake Road) to the lake. To reach Merrill Campground, continue left on Eagle Lake Road 1 mile or so. To reach Aspen, go right on Gallatin Road 1 mile or so past Eagle Campground.

KEY INFORMATION

Merrill or Aspen Campground, Lassen National Forest
Eagle Lake Ranger District
477-050 Eagle Lake Road
Susanville, CA 96130

Operated by: U.S. Forest Service

Information: (530) 257-4188, (530) 825-3454 (marina); www.r5.fs.fed.us/lassen

Open: May 15 through October 15 (depending on road and weather conditions)

Individual sites: Aspen has 26 sites; Merrill has 181 sites

Each site has: Picnic table, fire ring

Registration: At entrance; reserve by phone, (877) 444-6777, or online, www.reserveUSA.com

Facilities: Water, flush toilets

Parking: Near site at Aspen, at site at Merrill

Fee: $12 per site at Aspen Grove; $14–15 per site at Merrill; $8.65 nonrefundable reservation fee

Elevation: 5,100 feet

Restrictions:

Pets—On lesh only (no pets on trails)

Fires—In fireplace

Vehicles—No RVs at Aspen, RVs up to 32 feet at Merrill

THE CASCADES

BOULDER CREEK CAMPGROUND / LONE ROCK CAMPGROUND

Antelope Lake, Plumas National Forest, near Genesee

The drive into Antelope Lake through Taylorsville and Genesee is heart-breakingly bucolic. The road winds along little Beaver Creek through a Norman Rockwellian rural America. There are green pastures with cows belly deep in grass, small New England–style cottages, nearby weathered barns pushed over by the wind, willows down by the water, and tiny stores with creaking floorboards and 19th-century-style cash registers ornate as churches and as big as Yugos. You can buy ice and beer and cold cuts, and drive on, dreaming of a simpler past. Was it really simpler? I don't know, but the roll of the beautiful land certainly speaks to me.

Then you climb up along Beaver Creek to Antelope Lake and go left to the campgrounds. Boulder Creek and Lone Rock are basically the same campground. Lone Rock is down by the lake, and adjoining Boulder Creek Campground sits back on a ridge between Boulder Creek and an inlet of Antelope Lake.

Generally, everybody wants to be down on the water, so the campsites there at Lone Rock are called PLs, meaning priority lakeside sites. They cost more ($15) and can be reserved. As with most campgrounds, these sites by the lake are well used, designed for RVs (since RVers outnumber tent campers three to one), and are packed in together. Still, it's waterfront property. So to be by the lake, be sure to reserve—because there is a

CAMPGROUND RATINGS

Beauty:	★★★
Site privacy:	★★★★
Site spaciousness:	★★★
Quiet:	★★
Security:	★★★
Cleanliness/upkeep:	★★★★

Boulder Creek and Lone Rock Campgrounds are family camp-grounds, where folks come to enjoy the summer and the lake. There is limited hiking, but plenty of bicycling nearby.

steady supply of fishermen and retired folks with RVs or trailers who'll take these sites.

Remember, too, that the campers in this neck of the woods mostly come from Nevada. They come in big pickups with overpowered engines fit to tow a trailer and an aluminum boat, and still have power left over to run the air-conditioner cold enough to frost the brim of your Stetson. They're used to desert so they want to be by the water, but if you camp by a Nevada pickup,

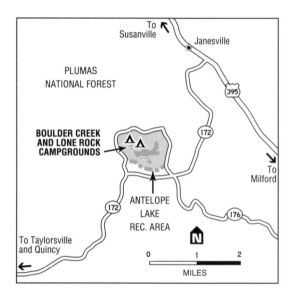

trailer, and boat, it's like tenting next to a scrap-metal lot.

So tent campers should best retreat from the water, to the ridge at Boulder Creek Campground. Here, camp under the pines on a thick bed of needles. The blue lake sparkles through the trees. Everything is clean and new in the summer, after shedding about 20 feet of winter snow. Only on big holiday weekends does Boulder Creek get much play, so don't plan on too many neighbors.

However, there are birds: cormorants, mergansers, grebes, coots, killdeer, geese, and great blue herons. I saw signs of beaver and what looked like an osprey. An owl (probably a great horned owl) hooted at night. I hiked up a logging spur on the south side of the lake and saw mule deer. I visited the log cabin and gravesites and the dam information site.

It seems Antelope Lake was not always a lake. Before California's Department of Water Resources built the dam in 1964 this was a wet, fertile valley. Maidu Native Americans came from their villages down near Taylorsville and Genesee in the summer to fish, hunt, and dig camus tubers and cattail rhizomes. They peeled back the cattail root to its core and made flour from it.

Early in the summer, they would steam the green-bloom cattail spikes to eat like corn on the cob. They would dry the cattail leaves and use these for weaving. The camus bulb was cooked in a stone-lined earth pit for 24 hours, then either eaten straightaway or dried in the sun for later consumption.

The advent of the forty-niners was the demise of the Maidu. Whites moved in, and the Antelope Lake area supplied the mining camps with forage, butter, and cheese. Visit the pioneer cabin and gravesites on the south side of the lake. Imagine what it was like for the folks living there. Only the lucky ones had log cabins with doors and windows. Most lived in tents or shacks with dirt floors and canvas ceilings. It was harsh. In fact, many people remembered the westward crossing more fondly than their life on the frontier. At least then they had traveling companions and dreams.

In the new land, before kerosene, there was no whale oil or tallow for candles. So the women used deer tallow. They papered the walls of their shacks with newspapers and reread the articles as they lived there. With no jars to can wild fruit, the women cooked the fruit, dried it, and hung it like beef jerky. Some learned to make flour from roots and acorns, if they had the stomach for it. Few did. And, indeed, many of the forty-niners found themselves living with Native American women because they just "plain et better."

On the other hand, a forty-niner would ride 70 miles to pay $20 in gold dust just to take a fresh-cooked biscuit from the hand of a white woman in a dress. Such was the strength of the men's longing for their lives back home.

KEY INFORMATION

Boulder Creek or Lone Rock Campground, Plumas National Forest
Mt. Hough Ranger District
39696 State Highway 70
Quincy, CA 95971

Operated by: U.S. Forest Service

Information: (530) 283-0555; www.r5.fs.fed.us/plumas

Open: May through October (depending on road and weather conditions)

Individual sites: Boulder Creek has 156 sites for tents or RVs; Lone Rock has 87 sites

Each site has: Picnic table, fireplace

Registration: At entrance; reserve by phone, (877) 444-6777, or online, www.reserveUSA.com

Facilities: Water, vault toilets

Parking: At individual site

Fee: $13; $15 for lakeside sites at Lone Rock; $8.65 nonrefundable reservation fee

Elevation: 5,000 feet

Restrictions:

Pets—On leash only

Fires—In fireplace

Vehicles—RVs up to 22 feet

Other—Don't leave food out; put food in car trunk

To get there: From Taylorsville take Beckwourth Genesee and Indian Creek Road (CR 172) northeast. Turn left at the dam, and go about 1 mile to the campgrounds.

THE CASCADES

CRATER LAKE CAMPGROUND

Crater Lake, Lassen National Forest, near Old Station

Crater Lake Campground has the most unexpected charm. You drive off Highway 44 across a railroad track toward a mountain in the distance. The mostly dirt road (only 7 miles) winds up around a volcanic cone. Rough only in places, the road brings you in a short time to the lip of the cone, and you look down on 27 acres of the prettiest little lake surrounded by aspens turning gold in the fall.

This is a small campground—only 17 campsites, and most of them are pitched wrong or too small for even small RVs, so this is prime tent camping. The sites are sprinkled up and down the loop to the lake's edge. Last time I was there, in September, we camped right on the lakeshore—no one else was there. The aspens (*Populus tremuloides*) were turning orange, yellow, and red against the black volcanic rock of the crater. What a beautiful spot!

California's little Crater Lake is part of the great lava plateau including, of course, Lassen Volcanic National Park and Lava Beds National Monument in Northern California and, in Oregon, Crater Lake National Park (not *our* Crater Lake). Lassen Peak last erupted in May 1914 for a seven-year cycle of sporadic outbursts. When will it go off again? Soon, in geologic time, but nobody knows.

Part of Crater Lake Campground's charm is being out in the middle of nowhere. The nearest reliable food supply is Susanville,

CAMPGROUND RATINGS

Beauty:	★★★★★
Site privacy:	★★★★
Site spaciousness:	★★★★
Quiet:	★★★★★
Security:	★★★★★
Cleanliness/upkeep:	★★★★

In the fall, when the aspens go gold, this little campground is pretty and fun. Lots of activities are available in the area.

an authentic cowboy town, which manages to have a modern supermarket and cash machine at the Bank of America. Gas, beer, and ice can be had at Old Station, west on Highway 44 at the junction of Highway 89. But if you want fresh meat, only Susanville will do.

Fishing on Crater Lake is pretty good, especially after it is stocked—and the 94-foot deep lake is host to freshwater crawdads that, in good years, can be trapped for a one crawdad/one bite meal. A ranger I spoke to says the

crawdad population goes up and down—in the 1980s the crawdads were especially prolific.

There is a hike around the lake. Back where the access road comes over the lip of the cone, there are several lumber roads heading out north. My wife and I walked all of them, then tried some cross-country trekking and found it easy going. You can easily hike through the patches of pine down into Harvey Valley or Pine Creek Valley. Still, I think of Crater Lake Campground as a one-night stop at an impossibly beautiful spot or a place to springboard by car to other adventures (like all of Lassen Volcanic National Park).

There is a beguiling island out in the middle of the lake. To get there, you need a watercraft. A canoe or kayak will do fine, as will an inflatable craft of some form. You can have lots of fun floating around the tiny lake fishing or reading, or sunbathing on the island with an occasional suicidal dip into the freezing water. On a nice day there is nothing better than the hot sun on your body and the feeling of the cold water through a few inches of insulating soft air compressed by the not-thick-enough sides of your blow-up raft or kayak (buy the inexpensive electric pump that runs off your car cigarette lighter).

Good hiking, biking, or horseback riding is found nearby on the Bizz Johnson Trail along the Susan River and the old Fernley & Lassen Railroad route from Susanville to Duck Lake, 4 miles north of Westwood. The Lassen National Forest Information Station, at the intersection of Route 44 and the Crater Lake Campground (FS 32N08), will cheerfully give you the Bizz Johnson Trail brochure, along with information on where to access the trail and where to rent bicycles or horses in Susanville.

Find more good hiking in Lassen Volcanic National Park at the Butte Lake trailheads, just a short way from Crater Lake Campground. Go out to Highway 44, then head west a few miles to FS 32N21. This road climbs 2.4 miles to Butte Creek Campground, then 4.1 miles to Butte Lake Ranger Station.

An easy hike from the north side of the Butte Lake parking lot is the trail to Bathtub Lake (warm, safe swimming). Climb about 500 yards and see two small lakes. The northernmost one is Bathtub, but both lakes will do for swimming. There are other trails from this Butte Lake area (get information at the Ranger Station) for more ambitious hikers.

For another great expedition take Highway 44 east toward Susanville, then A1 north to Eagle Lake. Go right on Gallatin Road, and find the beach and marina. A good boat and a motor runs about $50/day, and you could spend a week fishing for the singular lake trout and exploring the miles of shore.

KEY INFORMATION

Crater Lake Campground, Lassen National Forest Eagle Lake Ranger District
477-050 Eagle Lake Road
Susanville, CA 96130

Operated by: U.S. Forest Service

Information: (530) 257-4180; www.r5.fs.fed.us/lassen

Open: July through mid-September (depending on road and weather conditions)

Individual sites: 17 sites for tents or small campers

Each site has: Picnic table, fireplace

Registration: By entrance

Facilities: Well water, vault toilets

Parking: At individual site

Fee: $11

Elevation: 6,800 feet

Restrictions:

Pets—On leash only

Fires—In fireplace

Vehicles—No trailers over 20 feet

To get there: from Susanville, head 28 miles west on Highway 44 to the Lassen National Forest Information Center (and Bogard Work Center). Then drive north for 7 miles on Forest Service Road 32N08 to the Crater Lake Campground.

THE CASCADES

DOMINGO SPRINGS CAMPGROUND

Lassen National Forest, near Chester

Domingo Springs Campground is the yin of campgrounds—protected and feminine, down in the flowered and ferned shady marsh by the North Fork Feather River. Atop Lassen Volcanic National Park, you are close to major a supply source, Chester, and close to Lake Almanor for fishing, sailing, and swimming—but out of the way enough to camp in bucolic ease like a country squire.

There's good shopping at the supermarket in Chester—as well as decent cafes and restaurants right across the street. Get last-minute supplies and ease on into the campground when the shadows are long and Domingo Springs looks like a movie set, with its split-rail fences, rustic bridge, and wooded campsites.

All of the tent pitches are on soft ground, and most of them are backed into the woods. This campground is run by the University Foundation, California State University at Chico (like the other wonderful campgrounds at Eagle Lake), and it shows. Somebody has worried about how the campground looks and how it feels to camp there. Domingo Springs has an oriental-garden quality—magic.

The marsh around the springs is full of flowers. The trees around the campsites are full of staghorn lichens—a marriage of fungus and algae growing together. The green algae uses the sun and moisture to provide food for the lichen, while the fungus holds

CAMPGROUND RATINGS

Beauty:	★★★★★
Site privacy:	★★★★
Site spaciousness:	★★★★★
Quiet:	★★★★
Security:	★★★★★
Cleanliness/upkeep:	★★★★

Domingo Springs Campground represents the yin of campgrounds—cozy and idyllic, yet near the center of the earth—to the yang of nearby, busy Juniper Lake.

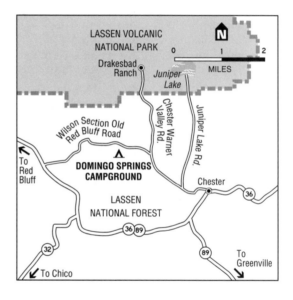

on to the tree, anchoring the lichen. The lichens grow just above the average level of the winter snowpack and do not hurt the trees.

Great bicycling is on the road by the campground called Wilson Lake Road/ Section Old Red Bluff Road. There is rarely any traffic on it, and it meanders a satisfactory distance between the Warner Valley Road and Highway 36, with a mountain bike access, Stump Ranch Road, a little ways to the west of the campground.

Domingo Springs Campground is right near the Pacific Crest Trail. Go west half a mile from the Domingo Springs Campground to find the trail where it crosses the road. We walked down into the gorge and across a bridge over the North Fork Feather River to picnic. The trail heads on another 8 or so miles to intersect Highway 36. The northern extension of the Pacific Crest Trail, on the other side of the Wilson Lake Road/Section Old Red Bluff Road, heads toward Drakesbad, going about 5 miles to Little Willow Lake.

The most fun at Domingo Springs is to sit around camp and watch the pattern of shadows and sunlight splashing on the marshy meadow. Get energetic and drive up the 7.8 miles of rough road to Juniper Lake. Here, find the other side of the Chinese universe, the yang, the bright and masculine. But there's no time to sit around and contemplate. Put on your boots and start hiking.

Juniper Lake is Lassen National Volcanic Park's biggest and deepest lake. It's also the least crowded. Most folks approach the park from the north. Perhaps they don't like that last jolting ride off the pavement to get here. In any event, you will have most of the hiking trails to yourself. From here, find trails up Mount Harkness and around Juniper Lake, as well as short hikes to Inspiration Point and Crystal Lake. Stop at the Ranger Station by the lake to get hiking information.

Another good trip is up to Warner Valley and legendary Drakesbad for a hike to Boiling Springs Lake. Drive back to Warner Valley Road and turn left. Go 9.9 miles into Lassen Volcanic National Park and Drakesbad (no shopping opportunities in Drakesbad, so come prepared). On the left you'll find the trailhead for Boiling Springs Lake. Pick up the trail guide brochure and start hiking (an easy mile's hike). Soon you will smell and hear Boiling Springs Lake—smell the hydrogen sulfide from gases and hear the "bumping" from the mud pots. Here's a hell to scare you straight. Then think about what created the whole Lassen area. Think about what's under the thin crust of earth you walk on.

Wonder why the folks around these parts are so cheery? Living on top of a bomb, they have to be. The last time Lassen Peak went off was in 1914, when it blew a huge mushroom cloud 7 miles into the air. This is an active volcanic area, and folks are always looking over their shoulder, expecting a Mount St. Helens–style eruption. After a while, people here get that plucky, self-sufficient attitude that the Brits perfected during the blitz.

Local Native Americans saw it another way. Atsugewi people tell about a warrior who dug into Lassen Peak to rescue his abducted lover. The mountain spirits admired his courage and invited him to marry his sweetheart and live inside the mountain with them. When Lassen Peak erupted, or when heavy storm clouds shrouded the peak, the Atsugewi said the warrior was smoking his peace pipe.

KEY INFORMATION

Domingo Springs Campground, Lassen National Forest
Almanor Ranger District
P.O. Box 767
Chester, CA 96020

Operated by: U.S. Forest Service

Information: (530) 258-2141; www.r5.fs.fed.us/lassen

Open: May 15 through October (phone ahead for weather)

Individual sites: 9 sites for tents only, 9 sites for tents or RVs

Each site has: Picnic table, fireplace

Registration: By entrance

Facilities: Water, vault toilets

Parking: At individual site

Fee: $12–13; prices set by concessionaire

Elevation: 5,200 feet

Restrictions:

Pets—On leash only

Fires—In fireplace

Vehicles—Trailers not recommended

Other—Check weather conditions and water availabilty

To get there: from Chester on Highway 36, turn onto Warner Valley Road by the fire station. Drive 0.6 mile to the first junction. Go left. Drive 5.5 miles to the second junction. Go left 2.3 miles to Domingo Springs Campground.

THE CASCADES

CASCADE RANGE

FOWLER'S CAMP CAMPGROUND

Shasta–Trinity National Forest, near McCloud

In the Spring, Fowler's Camp Campground is the most beautiful campground in Northern California. The woods are clean and new, and the McCloud River rushes by bright as a June bride. This is the time to come. In summer, when the sun is high in the sky and there's swimming and boating in the river, Fowler's Camp is still attractive and inviting, but by fall her skirts are a little dirty—the leaves on the trees are drooping and the ground is dusty and ready for a winter snow.

I proposed this theory to Toni and Pinky, the campground hosts on my arrival, and was told in no uncertain terms to wait a few weeks until the trees changed colors—then Fowler's Camp would be more beautiful than ever. "Oh, right," I countered, then beat a hasty retreat when a passing Gray Panther from Alabama, as her sweatshirt proudly proclaimed, set her dog upon me for such heresy. And rightfully so. For the leaves were starting to change on the shoulders of Mount Shasta, and fall brought new vibrance to Shasta–Trinity National Forest.

What's more, the McCloud is touted by its ever-faithful boosters, Toni and Pinky, as the most beautiful river in the world—the reason being the silt from Mount Shasta that turns the river a turquoise-green color. Besides, the McCloud River is renowned for trout fishing, and the McCloud runs right by Fowler's Camp Campground. At

CAMPGROUND RATINGS

Beauty:	★★★★★
Site privacy:	★★★★
Site spaciousness:	★★★★
Quiet:	★★
Security:	★★★
Cleanliness/upkeep:	★★★★

Fowler's Camp Campground is ravishing in the springtime. Come for the fishing and the McCloud River.

Fowler's Camp there is a five-fish limit. Bait, lure, and flies can be used. I spotted some kids fishing with Salmon eggs. The Gray Panther from Alabama swore by worms dug from the riverbank. (On the Lower Mc-Cloud River, only artificial flies and lures with pinched-down barbs can be used—and there's a two-fish limit.)

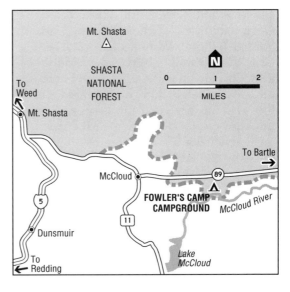

The swimming is good as well. At the swimming hole downstream from Fowler's Camp, by the Lower Falls Picnic Area, I found not only the beautiful falls and three friendly kayakers, but also a swimming hole complete with a ladder to ease into—and hurry out of—the water. I stuck my toe in. It wasn't bad. One woman offered that there were equally good swimming holes both above Fowler's Camp Campground and below the picnic area, which were more private and less filled with rampaging kids in the summer.

On the same kayaker's advice, I hiked up to Middle Falls. The trail heads upstream from Fowler's Camp Campground. I walked for about ten minutes before I heard water falling. Then I came around a turn in the trail and saw it—kind of a dribble on this September day, but a fisherman told me it goes like the Niagara in the spring, and kids climb up on the falls and jump down into the pool at the bottom. The drop had to be at least 50 yards. Even by teenaged logic, this is a frightening proposition.

I hurried on back to camp to unpack the car. I noticed that somebody put some thought into situating the sites. Most were private and well integrated into the woods, and each had a special level tent area set above the pitch. This feature could come in handy in a downpour, by directing the flood away from the tent floor. And the vault toilets were pristine! Fowler's Camp Campground's skirts weren't bedraggled after all.

In the morning, I headed off to the town of McCloud (the nearest supply source) to get ice for the cooler. I stopped at the Ranger Station and was directed to Soda Springs. Soda Springs, with natural springs surrounded by a split-railed trail, is about 3 miles south of McCloud on the Squaw Valley Road. According to the ranger, there used to be a town here with a hotel, curative baths, and a bottled soda water industry. Unfortunately, Soda Springs fell on hard times and vanished. Now there are eight beaver dams on the spot. This region was rich in beaver in the early 1800s, before they were trapped out. Beaver dams are good for a forest. First the dam creates a pond, then the pond inevitably silts in and becomes a rich meadow habitat for plants and animals.

I mentioned I was camping at Fowler's Camp Campground to the ranger, and while he waxed as proud as Toni and Pinky had, he also said that the best camping in the area was dispersed camping. Just stop at the Ranger Station and get fixed up with a permit and a map showing all the great places to go dispersed camping. Then he grinned and told me if he were on vacation, he would stay at the nearby, beautiful McCloud Guest House, in a 1907 mansion that once housed luminaries like President Herbert Hoover and Jean Harlowe (together?). He raved about the restaurant and it's prime rib. I went back to Fowler's Camp Campground and enjoyed a camping staple: corned beef hash with a fried egg—and ketchup, naturally.

KEY INFORMATION

Fowler's Camp Campground, Shasta–Trinity National Forests

McCloud Ranger District

P.O. Box 1620

McCloud, CA 06957

Operated by: U.S. Forest Service

Information: (530) 964-2184; www.r5.fs.fed.us/ shastatrinity

Open: May through November (depending on road and weather conditions)

Individual sites: 39 sites for tents or RVs and trailers

Each site has: Picnic table, fireplace/camp stove, open fire pit with grate

Registration: At entrance

Facilities: Water, vault toilets

Parking: At individual site

Fee: $12

Elevation: 3,600 feet

Restrictions:

Pets—On leash only

Fires—In fireplace only

Vehicles—RVs up to 30 feet

Other—Don't leave food out

To get there: from McCloud, drive east on Highway 89 for 5.5 miles to the campground entrance on the right-hand side of the road. It is well signed.

THE CASCADES

HEMLOCK CAMPGROUND

Medicine Lake, Modoc National Forest, near Bartle

L ast time my wife and I came into Hemlock Campground on Medicine Lake, all we could see were black clouds over the mountain, stretching off as far as Washington State according to the radio weather reports. By the time we reached the lake, the tulle fog was blowing in with rain not too far behind it. We got our tent up, our gear stowed, the flashlights turned on, and the travel Scrabble game set up before the rain turned to blinding sleet. It blew and blew, then the sleet turned to snow, and we put in earplugs so we wouldn't hear the flapping of the tent fly. And then it was morning, and the sun was blazing off blue Medicine Lake and the fish were jumping.

Medicine Lake is beautiful. Hemlock Campground is the first of the three campgrounds you come to on the east side of the lake. After Hemlock you reach A. H. Hogue, then Medicine Lake. All three are fine campgrounds. Hemlock is more geared to tents, with fewer flat places to park RVs. A. H. Hogue, is a little flatter but still favors tents. Flat Medicine Lake Campground attracts the majority of the RVs and trailers.

Hemlock Campground is nearest the beach and boat launch. God knows how, but the beach is composed of actual white sand. It even has a natural kiddie pool, protected by a sandbar. Medicine Lake does allow motorboats, but felicitously water-skiers are only permitted on the lake

CAMPGROUND RATINGS

Beauty:	★★★★★
Site privacy:	★★★★★
Site spaciousness:	★★★★★
Quiet:	★★★★
Security:	★★★★
Cleanliness/upkeep:	★★★★

A beautiful place to stay in the summer to fish and swim and enjoy nearby Lava Beds National Monument for good hiking and cave exploring.

between 10 A.M. and 4 P.M. This leaves fishermen free to troll in the morning and evening for the more than 100,000 brook trout stocked in the lake every year.

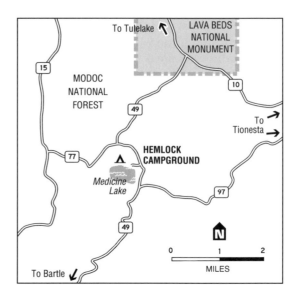

To Tulelake

LAVA BEDS NATIONAL MONUMENT

MODOC NATIONAL FOREST

15

49

10

To Tionesta

77

HEMLOCK CAMPGROUND

Medicine Lake

97

49

N

0   1   2

MILES

To Bartle

As we found out the hard way, the Modoc plateau has a mercurial nature. Its climate is "dry continental," meaning nasty. The weather can change between freezing and sweltering in a whisker. In August titanic thunderstorms on the horizon bring impressive lightning but little rain. In winter the wind blows bitter cold.

Pack a bathing suit and a ski jacket. You never know what to expect up here.

This is an incredibly dramatic landscape. No wonder: Hemlock Campground sits atop a 100-square-mile volcano—more massive than Mount Shasta. You don't notice it because the Medicine Lake Highlands come on you as slowly as the curve of the sea. Go see Mammoth Crater north of Medicine Lake to look inside the belly of the beast. And Mammoth Crater is not even the mouth of the volcano, which is actually 6 miles south near Medicine Lake.

Take a couple of hours and hike around Medicine Lake. Take a quick detour on the trail by the Medicine Lake Campground to see Little Medicine Lake. The road past the campgrounds goes halfway around the lake. After that, just follow the lake. You'll find great places to picnic. It's not a bad idea to bring some bad-weather gear, just in case. Those little pocket raincoats they sell in the camping stores can come in handy. Little more than a light garbage bag, they are welcome companions when the skies open up.

Glass Mountain is a fun place to visit, reached via a good, short hike. Turn right out of Hemlock Campground. Drive south to Forest Service Road 97. Go left for 6 miles, passing the first sign for Glass Mountain. Take the second left on FS 43N99. There isn't any real trail—just hike around. Part of this place is privately owned, so mind the signs. What you find here is dacite (the gray-colored stuff) and rhyolitic obsidian (the sharp, shiny stuff). The Modocs came up here often to gather obsidian to make arrowheads, spearheads, and tools to use and trade with Native Americans from as far away as the coast.

Other great hikes await down in Lava Beds National Monument. You have to explore Captain Jack's Stronghold (get the Lava Beds National Monument brochure for the map to the park, and cough up a quarter for the "Captain Jack's Stronghold" Historical Trail brochure). Try to find out how Captain Jack retreated and follow the trail. The Thomas Wright Trail (white man's folly) is another hour's hike as well as the Schonchin Butte Trail (short but steep). The Whitney Butte Trail is a day trip, so bring lunch and enjoy yourself. You end up on the edge of Callahan Lava Flow. In 1969, skeptics accused NASA of filming the lunar landing there. See for yourself.

There are two ways to get to Lava Beds National Monument. Go north on FS 49, which is the bumpy way (17 miles). Or take FS 97 to FS 10 near Timber Mountain Store at Tionesta (36 miles—the smoother way). They both take about the same time. It's best to take the corduroy road going downhill, then come back the long way and get gas, ice, and cold drinks at the store. The next nearest supply is at the supermarket in Tulelake.

KEY INFORMATION

Hemlock Campground, Modoc National Forest
Doublehead Ranger District
P.O. Box 369
Tulelake, CA 96134

Operated by: U.S. Forest Service

Information: (530) 667-2246, (530) 233-5811; www.r5.fs.fed.us/medoc

Open: July through October (depending on road and weather conditions)

Individual sites: 19 sites for tents or small RVs

Each site has: Picnic table, fireplace

Registration: At entrance

Facilities: Water, pit toilets

Parking: At individual site

Fee: $7 per vehicle per night

Elevation: 6,700 feet

Restrictions:

Pets—On leash only

Fires—In fireplace

Vehicles—RVs up to 22 feet

Other—Don't leave food out

To **get there:** from Bartle on Highway 89, head northeast up Powder Hill Road (Forest Service Road 49) to Medicine Lake Road. Then go left to the Hemlock Campground.

THE CASCADES

INDIAN WELL CAMPGROUND

Lava Beds National Monument, near Tulelake

For hundreds of years people have camped on the flat at Indian Well. This is the only flat, open ground nearby. Soft pumice covers most of the rocks, so it is easy to pitch a shelter and sleep on the ground. The flat is up high enough so visitors can see for miles. And there is water in the Indian Well Cave, visible by daylight.

The first campers here, the Modocs and their ancestors, lived north of the lava beds along Tule and Lower Klamath Lakes, subsisting on waterfowl, water-lily seeds, and fish, and cutting the tule reeds for bedding, hats, and canoes. In the fall, the Modoc camped at Indian Well on their way to the mountains to hunt bear, bighorn sheep, and pronghorn antelope and harvest manzanita, berries, and pine nuts. The Modoc were fierce and fought with the Pit River people and the Klamath to keep their rich lands. Then settlers came, and the Modoc fought hard against them and the U.S. Army. They lost—Modoc culture was erradicated to make way for ranchers.

Time has marched on, and many of the lakes the Modoc fished from have been drained; the pronghorn herds are gone; and the bunchgrass the bighorn ate has given way to cheatgrass (an exotic plant from Asia). But we can still come here and camp, explore the Modoc's sacred lava tube caves, hike among the sage and the rabbit bush blooming yellow in the fall, and imagine a time when this area was lit only by fire.

CAMPGROUND RATINGS

Beauty:	★★★★★
Site privacy:	★★★★
Site spaciousness:	★★★
Quiet:	★★★★★
Security:	★★★★★
Cleanliness/upkeep:	★★★★★

Lava Beds National Monument is a true destination campground. This is the most awesome spot in Northern California.

Lava Beds National Monument first shocks you, then rewards you. The land seems desolate and savage. The lava rocks cut like razors. Then you spot the vegetation, and find the land is rich and full of life. Here the continental plates were pulled apart, so magma rose up from the interior of the earth to form this land. There remain cinder cones, shield volcanoes, strato-volcanoes, spatter cones, chimneys, Pahoehoe lava, and lava flow caves.

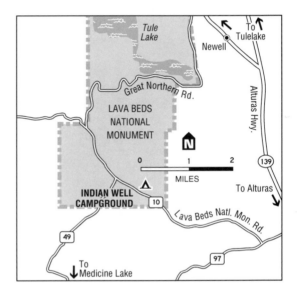

I love Lava Beds National Monument. Of all my family's western trips when I was a child, I remember Lava Beds the best. Even as a little kid, I was awed at the elemental violence that created this land and how quickly the vegetation took over to give life. What an amazing place! From the campground, you can hike miles over the rock along Three Sisters Trail. Or drop down into any one of Lava Bed's caves with a flashlight and map. The whole area is an incredible adventure, and visitors are expected to explore responsibly by themselves.

The Visitor Center is half a mile away from the campground, and there you can buy the Lava Beds Caves map book ($4.50). The Park Headquarters also lends flashlights if you need to supplement your own. Going into the caves is no joke. Bring warm clothes (cold air collects in the caves). A hard hat for your head is a good idea, but at least wear a cloth hat. Never go alone, and be sure to tell somebody responsible which cave you are going to explore and when you are going to get back. Gloves, knee pads, a first-aid kit, and food and water are musts if you go cave exploring whole hog—most people get bitten by cave exploration and can't stop.

Come prepared for hot and cold camping. Even in the summer, Lava Beds can be cold, and a stiff wind can make a cool day freezing. The dry continental climate of the Modoc Plateau is ferocious. The interiors of the lava caves are always cold. It can be very dry. Bring Chap Stick and moisturing lotion. Bring a good hat with a drawstring to hold it on in the wind. Bring earplugs to use at night so that you won't lose any sleep hearing the tent flapping. Bring shorts and a T-shirt too, because with all the preparation for bad weather, the clime is bound to be balmy.

During the season, the campsite has piped water. After that, there is water available at the Visitor Center up the road. So remember to bring water containers. I like the collapsible plastic water jugs available in most camping stores, although water stored too long in them gets a plastic taste. There is no food available at the Visitor Center. Buy real food at Tulelake (like a set from *Last Picture Show*), which actually has a motel. Ice, beer, and hot dogs are available at rustic Tionesta (you have to go a few hundred yards off the road). Don't pass up either town without getting gas—they have the only pumps for miles.

Season permitting, try to camp up on the Medicine Lake Volcano, which blew off lava, gas, and cinders for a million years to give us the lava beds. In addition to three campgrounds, there's a good beach, decent fishing, and Mammoth Crater and Glass Mountain.

To get there: from Tulelake, drive south on Highway 39. Before Newell, go right on the Great Northern Road, and drive 27 miles to the Lava Beds National Monument Visitor Center. The entrance to the Indian Well Campground is across from the Visitor Center.

KEY INFORMATION

Indian Well Campground, Lava Beds National Monument Supervisor
Box 867
Tulelake, CA 96134

Operated by: National Park Service

Information: (530) 667-2282 ext. 230; www.nps.gov/labe

Open: All year

Individual sites: 40 sites for tents, pickup campers, or small trailers; 1 group site for 14–40 people

Each site has: Picnic table, fireplace

Registration: At entrance

Facilities: Water and flush toilets May 15 through October 15; water at Visitor Center and pit toilets during the rest of year

Parking: At individual site

Fee: $4 (per vehicle) to enter Monument; $10 per night when piped water is available; $6 in the winter when water is turned off

Elevation: 4,200 feet

Restrictions:

Pets—On leash only

Fires—In fireplace

Vehicles—Pickup campers or small trailers only; no RVs

Other—14-day stay limit

THE CASCADES

JUNIPER LAKE CAMPGROUND

Juniper Lake, Lassen Volcanic National Park, near Chester

Come to Lassen Volcanic National Park and camp at Juniper Lake Campground because it offers the least crowded camping, hiking, and fishing in the park. Juniper Lake, blue and deep, is by Lassen Peak, Mount Harkness, and Saddle Mountain. Up until recently, in geologic time, Juniper Lake wasn't even a lake. About 200,000 years ago, all that was here was a depression with hundreds of feet of ice cap and icy fingers heading down into Warner Valley. The area warmed up, and a stream ran through the basin. Nearby volcanic Mount Harkness hadn't happened, but when it did, it dammed up the south part of the basin, and—voilà!—Juniper Lake was born.

The last 8 miles into the Juniper Lake Campground are not great driving, but if you go slowly you can make it in any kind of vehicle. You just have to take your time and be careful. Plan on taking an hour to make that last 8 miles. Once you scale down your expectations, rough road traveling becomes enjoyable. Suddenly you can see the trees and the birds instead of a rushing green blur. Let about five pounds of air out of each tire if you want to stop your dentures from rattling. And remember, a nasty road is what keeps Juniper Lake from being a tourist hotspot. This is deliberate policy. Years ago, the Lassen Volcanic National Park decided not to stock its lakes and not to fix up its roads, hoping to

CAMPGROUND RATINGS

Beauty:	★★★★★
Site privacy:	★★★★
Site spaciousness:	★★★★★
Quiet:	★★★★★
Security:	★★★★★
Cleanliness/upkeep:	★★★★★

Juniper Lake Campground is the most pristine in Lassen Volcanic National Park. But it is the hardest to get to—so come prepared.

staunch the stampede and keep the park as pristine as possible.

Do all your shopping in Chester before you drive into Juniper Lake, because you won't want to pop out for hot dog buns. Phone the park in advance to find out if there is water at the campground. The weather around here is unpredictable, and the rangers won't turn on the water if the pipes might freeze. If there's no water at the park, you'll need to bring in at least a gallon of water per person per day, or a

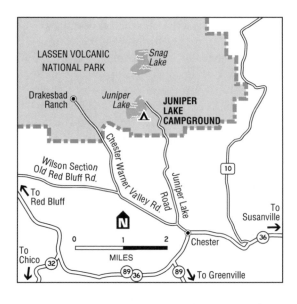

water-filter unit (about $60 at camping stores). Filtering is lots of work as well—it takes a ton of pumping to filter out a quart of water.

Come prepared for any kind of weather. At any time, Juniper Lake can be freezing or like August on the Riviera. Bring winter sleeping bags with a sheet—use the sheet over you and lie on the bag if it is hot. If it's cold, crawl into the warm sleeping bag.

Be sure to hike up to Crystal Lake. This hike is only about half a mile, but it is a killer. When you arrive, you'll need a swim regardless of the weather. Fortunately, Crystal Lake is warm! Why? I don't know. Juniper Lake is gelid. Maybe Crystal Lake is warm because it is on a south-facing slope. Bring a lunch and stay all day. Some say Crystal Lake has trout—I didn't see anyone catch anything, but folks were fishing.

The hike up Mount Harkness is another steep climb (about 4 miles round-trip). Catch the trail right from the campground. Hike up through the firs and pines until the woods open up into slopes of gray rock—lava from Mount Harkness. Keep hiking up until you hit the cinder cone, and then head west, up through hemlocks to the ridge. From there it's up another ten minutes to the fire lookout on the rim. From the lookout you can see just about the whole park. On the way back, a loop trail goes left and down to Juniper Lake. When you hit the lake, head east back to the campground. This loop is a another mile or two longer than going back the way you came in.

Another good hike is around Juniper Lake, and this is more of a trek than one would expect. We underestimated the distance and forgot a lunch. The whole loop is about 6 miles, and there is enough up and down that we took three hard hours to complete the trail/cottage access road back to Juniper Lake Campground. There is a rocky point on the Mount Harkness end of the lake, where we went swimming in the cold water. After involuntary gasps of shock came welcome numbness and then the exhilaration that keeps all those Nordic countries on their toes.

I heartily recommend bringing any rubber flotation device you can afford that will get your highly vulnerable body on the gorgeous blue lake but definitely out of the water. Think Big 5's Sevylor $50 blowups with an air pump powerred by your vehicle's cigarette lighter. Never set your device down on sharp shale or pine needles—and come prepared with a repair kit.

To get there: from Chester on Highway 36, turn on Warner Valley Road by the fire station. Drive 0.6 mile to the first junction. Turn right onto Juniper Lake Road and go 11 miles to the Juniper Lake Campground on your left.

KEY INFORMATION

Juniper Lake Campground, Lassen Volcanic National Park
Superintendent
P.O. Box 100
Mineral, CA 96063-0100

Operated by: National Park Service

Information: (530) 595-4444; www.nps.gov/lavo

Open: June through September (phone ahead for weather)

Individual sites: 18 sites for tents

Each site has: Picnic table, fir ring, bear box

Registration: By entrance

Facilities: Water in warm weather only (phone ahead), vault toilets

Parking: At individual site

Fee: $10 park entrance fee (good for 7 days); $10 camping fee

Elevation: 6,792 feet

Restrictions:

Pets—On leash only; no pets on trails

Fires—In fire ring

Vehicles—Small campers only; no RVs

Other—Check for weather and use bear boxes; rough, dirt road not recommended for trailers

THE CASCADES

McARTHUR-BURNEY FALLS MEMORIAL STATE PARK

Near Burney

Come to McArthur-Burney Memorial Falls State Park in the summer armed with reservations and children. You need reservations to get a campsite and children to play with all the other kids teeming the campsites, hiking the trails, and cavorting on the beautiful beach by the marina. However, in the fall or spring, McArthur-Burney offers peace and quiet. It is a premium state park with good swimming, fishing, and hiking, as well as comfortable camping with hot showers.

Lake Britton is a reservoir but is uniquely fed (design courtesy of Ma Nature) by an underground spring that fills the reservoir and keeps the 129-foot Burney Falls flowing. Teddy Roosevelt called the falls the Eighth Wonder of the World. Back East in the Finger Lakes we have falls like Burney all over the place, but we don't have black swifts building rare inland nests of lichens on the cliffs. Nor do we have water ouzels (*Cinclus mexicanus*) diving into the creek to walk along the bottom while feeding. The birds hold their wings partially open. The current pressing on their wings helps to hold them down. They can go as deep as 20 feet and stay down for a minute before shooting up into the sky like a rocket.

On Lake Britton, which has good fishing (rent canoes, paddleboats, and motorboats at the park marina), look for great blue herons, Canada geese, and a multitude of ducks and grebes. Bald eagles visit in the

CAMPGROUND RATINGS

Beauty:	★★★★★
Site privacy:	★★★
Site spaciousness:	★★★★★
Quiet:	★★★
Security:	★★★★★
Cleanliness/upkeep:	★★★★

This is the Queen of Northern California State Campgrounds. Teddy Roosevelt called the nearby falls the Eighth Wonder of the World.

winter, when the weather gets too rough for them up in Canada. In the campground, we saw red-headed woodpeckers, evening grosbeaks, and a host of other birds. At night we heard the great horned owl, a creature with a five-feet wingspan capable of kidnapping a small dog. Yet the owl is constantly bullied by crows. How? Tough and clever, crows attack together.

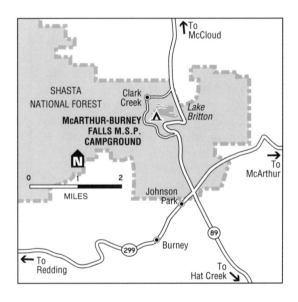

Around the campground you will find some good hikes—especially the popular Fall Creek Trail. This is a 1.2-mile self-guided interpretive loop that tours the creek canyon. Avoid this trail at all costs in the summer except to access the trail that runs down the canyon to the beach on Lake Britton. Other times, this loop is astonishingly beautiful.

Another quick walk is up the Headwaters Trail to the underground spring and reservoir revered by the Ilmawi Native Americans living in nearby villages. The Ilmawi dug deep pits in deer trails to trap big game, so the first whites called the Ilmawi the Pit Indians. The underground spring and reservoir are the result of all the vulcanism in the area. Lava rock is all over the place, and sometimes water percolates through the lava rock and is trapped in underground rivers and reservoirs, or aquifers. One of these aquifers feeds Burney Creek and Burney Falls. Sometimes Burney Creek is dry for a half-mile above the falls, but the falls flow year-round, fed by a subterranian source.

Good bicycling is found on the Old Highway Road that runs around the west side of Lake Britton (not Highway 89). This road takes off from Highway 89 about a half-mile south of the McArthur-Burney Falls Memorial State Park entrance. It is a decent ride as far as the Cross Creek Lodge (a favorite hideout of Al Capone's), but then the road starts climbing earnestly up to Highway 89. Best to turn around at the lodge.

The lovely campsites at McArthur-Burney were constructed by the CCC in the 1930s. Many of them back into the canyon rim, where a trail heads down to the lake. With plenty of good pitch space, this is prime tent camping.

See how few bushes there are. At first I thought they were pruned by a busy ranger. Not so, a friendly ranger informed me that rainfall on the porous basalt rock quickly soaks too deep for the shallow roots of most bushes—another effect of vulcanism. She also gave me some good advice. When phoning for reservations, request a tent-trailer site. It seems there are 103 tent-trailer sites but only 25 tent sites, so your chances of getting a reservation are vastly improved. Upon arrival, you may ask the ranger to transfer to a tent site if one is available.

If popular McArthur-Burney is full, camp at Northshore, a Pacific Gas & Electric campground just around the lake. This small lakeshore campground (30 sites and no reservations) always feels peaceful. Like most PG&E campgrounds, Northshore is clean, well run, and beautiful in an understated way. To reach Northshore, just turn left out of the main gate of McArthur-Burney and drive north on Highway 89 around the east shore of Lake Britton. Find Clarks Creek Road (otherwise known as Old Highway Road) on the left and drive 0.9 mile to the entrance on the left and continue a mile down the winding road.

Lake Britton is enchanting. Mist purls down from the hills and spills over the water, and you expect a scene from a James Fenimore Cooper novel to materialize before your astonished eyes.

KEY INFORMATION

McArthur-Burney Memorial Falls State Park
24898 Highway 89
Burney, CA 96013

Operated by: California Department of Parks and Recreation

Information: (530) 335-2777; http://parks.ca.gov

Open: All year; one loop with 20 sites open through winter

Individual sites: 25 sites for tents only, 103 sites for tents or RVs up to 32 feet

Each site has: Picnic table, fireplace, food storage

Registration: By entrance; reserve by phone, (800) 444-7275, or online, www.reserveamerica.com

Facilities: Water, flush toilets, coin-operated showers, wood for sale, dump stations

Parking: At individual site

Fee: $12; $8.65 nonrefundable reservation fee

Elevation: 2,800 feet

Restrictions:

Pets—On leash only

Fires—In fireplace

Vehicles—RVs up to 32 feet

Other—Memorial Day to Labor Day, reservations required

To get there: from Burney, drive east on Highway 299 until it intersects with Highway 89. Drive north to the McArthur-Burney Memorial Falls State Park Entrance.

THE CASCADES

MILL CREEK FALLS CAMPGROUND / BLUE LAKE CAMPGROUND

South Warner Wilderness Area, Modoc National Forest, near Likely

These two campgrounds are out in the middle of nowhere—the South Warner Wilderness is tucked away in California's northeastern corner. It takes forever to get here, but the drive is stunningly beautiful and well worth the effort. Nowhere in the West do you find an area so pristine and so untrammeled. South Warner is big sky country. There are real cowboys, real Native Americans, and real Thai food. Real Thai food? You bet, partner!

As fraternal twins often are, Mill Creek Falls and Blue Lake Campgrounds are like day and night. Blue Lake Campground is big and bustling with a boat launch and plenty of fishermen. However, a well-designed campground—like a tiered wedding cake on a high point going out into Blue Lake—gives the campsites a private,

CAMPGROUND RATINGS
Mill Creek Falls

Beauty:	★★★★★
Site privacy:	★★★★
Site spaciousness:	★★★★★
Quiet:	★★★★★
Security:	★★★★★
Cleanliness/upkeep:	★★★★★

CAMPGROUND RATINGS
Blue lake

Beauty:	★★★★
Site privacy:	★★★★★
Site spaciousness:	★★★★★
Quiet:	★
Security:	★★★
Cleanliness/upkeep:	★★★★★

Come to the pristine Warner Wilderness and eat Thai food in historic Alturas. A bit of a safari, this is the one trip you will never regret.

secluded feeling. You are separated from your neighbors, and everywhere you look, there are the bright flashes of blue from natural Blue Lake. Come here if you have a boat and want to go fishing (5 mph speed limit).

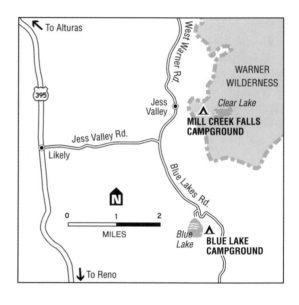

I talked with some of the other campers and fishermen. They were caught their limit of planted rainbow trout but talked about some big brown trout weighing 15 pounds. One old-timer said he hooked one earlier that summer and it towed him around the lake.

The only fly in the ointment was a helicopter we woke to in the morning. It seems a lumber company is timbering the shores of Blue Lake and pulling the trees out by air. It was horrible. We packed up and left for Mill Creek Falls Campground.

Mill Creek Falls Campground is the best destination in the area for hikers and hiking fishermen. A smaller campground, the sites are set in a hollow under the pines. It is clean and intimate. The smell of the woods is almost overwhelming. A short walk away (maybe a mile) is Clear Lake. A natural lake, formed by a landslide, Clear Lake has some big brown trout as well, though not in the same class as Blue Lake. But here you can enjoy solitude, the pines and rocks reflecting off the water, and the nice little jaunt to a place where you won't see or hear the internal combustion engine (although there is no guarantee the Forest Service won't let them cut around Mill Creek Falls—write your congressperson).

To reach Clear Lake, find the trailhead right across from campsite 10 by a parking area. There's a display map, but it's best to come equipped with your own South Warner Wilderness–Modoc National Forest map in case you opt to hike on past Clear Lake. With your fishing rod in your hand, head up the trail. You come to a sign pointing left to Mill Creek Falls. It's a 200-yard diversion to admire the falls. Back on the main trail, carry on to Clear Lake. A trail loop goes left around the lake. The beautiful lake is close enough to Mill Creek Falls Campground that you can hike up for a quick lunch, or even a sundowner, and still make it back to camp with the last light.

A great fishing hike heads up Mill Creek from the Soup Springs Trailhead. Drive out of Mill Creek Falls Campground, and take a right on West Warner Road. Then take another right on Forest Service Road 40N24, and find the Soup Springs Trailhead on your right. Hike up over a hill into Mill Creek Valley. Here you will hit Mill Creek and soon see where it runs into Slide Creek Trail. Go left on the Mill Creek Trail, and head up the left side of Mill Creek for a couple of miles (the fishing here can be quite good). If you are truly ambitious, and have the time, continue another 4 miles to the summit of Warren Peak.

The nearest supply is in the town of Likely, which has gas, ice, and other basic stuff at the corner store. But if you need meat or groceries, then head on up to Alturas. This place is hopping! Not only does Alturas have the county's only two traffic lights, a great museum filled with esoteric exhibits, the wild-and-woolly Niles Hotel on Main Street, and a supermarket on Highway 299 coming into town, but it's also home to Nipas—a Thai/French/California-cuisine restaurant run by genuine Thai people. Nipas was mobbed when we arrived in town by all the locals as well as a blue-rinse, elderly ladies' social group. It was wild!

KEY INFORMATION

Mill Creek Falls or Blue Lake Campground

Warner Mountain Ranger District

P.O. Box 220

Cedarville, CA 96104

Operated by: U.S. Forest Service

Information: (530) 279-2687; www.r5.fs.fed.us/medoc

Open: May through November or first snow (phone ahead for weather)

Individual sites: Mill Creek Falls has 19 sites; Blue Lake has 48 sites, 19 with RV hook-ups

Each site has: Picnic table, fireplace

Registration: By entrance

Facilities: Water, vault toilets

Parking: At individual site

Fee: Blue Lake, $7; Mill Creek, $6

Elevation: Blue Lake 6,000 ft.; Mill Creek 5,700 feet

Restrictions:

Pets—On leash only

Fires—In fireplace

Vehicles—RVs up to 22 feet

Other—Check for weather and for water availability

To get there: drive 17 miles south of Alturas on U.S. 395 to Likely. Go left on Jess Valley Road for 9 miles to where the road forks. Go left at this fork for 2.5 miles, bear right, and go 2 miles to the Mill Creek Falls Campground. Go right at this fork, and drive 7 miles on Blue Lake Road to another right turn. Go 2 miles here to Blue Lake Campground.

THE CASCADES

SILVER BOWL CAMPGROUND / ROCKY KNOLL CAMPGROUND

Lassen National Forest, near Westwood

Silver Bowl and Rocky Knoll Campgrounds on stunning Silver Lake in the Caribou Wilderness (don't expect to see any caribou) are basically the same campground. Rocky Knoll Campground is by the base of Silver Lake, where the low-lying land by the stream is marshy. The campsites are very private—well ringed by foliage on rich, red-clay earth. Nearby is the Rocky Knoll Picnic Grounds, which has a little beach area bordered by aspens.

Just a half-mile away on the right (north) side of the lake is Silver Bowl Campground, where huge silver cliffs fall away to the incredibly blue-green water. (Silver Lake is named, naturally, for the sheer siver cliffs, not the color of the water.) Although Rocky Knoll is beautiful in spring and fall with that rich fen feeling, it has a tendency to be a bit buggy when the weather heats up in July. I prefer Silver Bowl because it is drier and tempts you with flashes of blue water through the pines. Then you climb up over the point and see the dramatic silver cliffs rising from the edge of the shore. Silver Bowl Picnic Area is just east of the campground along the lake, with great opportunities for sitting at the tables watching the sun dip down over the cliffs.

This lake has a friendly pioneer feeling. The cabins along the lake—the Silver Lake Summer Homes—are connected to the Forest Service and built in a rugged, outdoorsy

CAMPGROUND RATINGS

Beauty:	★★★★★
Site privacy:	★★★★★
Site spaciousness:	★★★★
Quiet:	★★★★★
Security:	★★★★★
Cleanliness/upkeep:	★★★★

These two campgrounds are little known to outsiders. Beautiful lakes, easy hiking, and good back-country fishing.

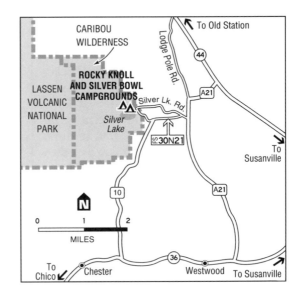

way. Silver Lake is off the beaten track and used mostly by local folks or longtimers, so you get a very safe feeling. Not being geared to the tourist trade, the Silver Lake area definitely suffers from a lack of signs telling the newcomer where to go.

The dirt access road to Silver Lake off A21 was marked the last time I was in the territory by a paper plate nailed to a tree. So you must watch your mileage gauge carefully to mark off the 12.5 miles north on A21 from Westwood. Once you arrive at Silver Lake, grope your way around the bottom of the lake to Rocky Knoll or north around the lake to Silver Bowl. Keep the faith: you will arrive at the campground you seek, because that's all there is out there. Just don't take the signed dirt road to Caribou Lake unless you do intend to go there.

Once you get over directional anxiety, get a campsite and look around—see what a beautiful place Caribou Wilderness is! The land is on a volcanic plateau filled with cinder cones and crater peaks with dozens of little lakes (nearby Thousand Lakes Wilderness has few lakes, and no caribou, either) with pretty good fishing. Most of what you see are lodgepole pine mixed with Jeffrey pine, fir, and hemlock. Look for bald eagles, ospreys, mergansers, and grebes.

I was told by a friendly ranger to look for the pine marten, which is often mistaken for a large squirrel. On closer inspection it is supposed to look like a house cat with a short, bushy tail. I was on alert but only scared up an adolescent bear that was worrying the garbage cans at Silver Bowl Campground.

The same ranger gave me the word about Silver Lake fishing. It is good after being stocked. But the best fishing is in the small lakes you can hike to. This information was verified by several hiking fishermen I queried during our visit, including one individual camping near us who was frying several specimens up in his pan for dinner.

Good hiking from Silver Bowl and Rocky Knoll Campgrounds starts from the Caribou Lake trailhead about 0.3 mile north from Silver Bowl Campground. (There is a trail from the Silver Bowl Campground loop to the trailhead, but take the road first to orient yourself, since this area is easy to get lost in because it has few visible landmarks.) From here you can access trails to Cowboy Lake, Emerald Lake, Jewel Lake, Eleanor Lake, and so on. Best to get a good topo map from any Ranger Station on the way in.

The weather in Caribou Wilderness can get very cold in spring and fall, so dress accordingly and take some extra clothes when you hike. It can rain like hell here, too, so plan for that. Weatherproof the inside seams of your tent before you leave home. Otherwise, plan on tributaries of the nearby Susan River running through your tent when it rains. Bring a tarp to pitch your tent on. Fix the tarp so that when the water wants to pool under your tent it will go under the tarp instead. Bring a garden trowel to dig a ditch around your tent. If the weather threatens, it is much more fun to dig before it is raining cats and dogs than afterwards, when you're mad as a wet hen.

If you get tired of Silver Lake, try the other campgrounds around Lassen Volcanic National Park—Warner Valley, Domingo Springs, Juniper Lake, and Crater Lake—because they are among the best in the West.

KEY INFORMATION

Silver Bowl or Rocky Knoll Campground, Lassen National Forest
Almanor Ranger District
P.O. Box 676
Chester, CA 96020

Operated by: U.S. Forest Service

Information: (530) 258-2141; www.r5.fs.fed.us/lassen

Open: May 1 through November 1 (weather permitting)

Individual sites: Silver Bowl— 18 sites for tents or RVs; Rocky Knoll—18 sites for tents or RVs

Each site has: Picnic table, fireplace, campfire rings

Registration: By entrance

Facilities: Water, vault toilets

Parking: At individual site

Fee: $11

Elevation: 6,000 feet

Restrictions:

Pets—On leash only

Fires—In fireplace

Vehicles—RVs up to 26 feet

Other—Keep food in car trunk

To get there: from Westwood, drive 12.5 miles north on A21. Turn left on Silver Lake Road, and drive 7.5 miles on a graded dirt road to the campgrounds. The Rocky Knoll Campground is at the base of Silver Lake. Silver Bowl Campground is 0.5 mile away on the north side of Silver Lake.

THE CASCADES

WARNER VALLEY CAMPGROUND

Lassen Volcanic National Park, near Chester

Warner Valley Campground is a great place to come! Catering to tent campers (the road in is not recommended for trailers), there aren't even any bears (thanks to the new bear boxes). There is a Ranger Station a mile back down the road. There's the resort a few hundred yards up the road. The trails are spectacular. Hot Springs Creek gurgles by the campground, lulling the tent camper to sleep. The creek swimming is great. The sites are shaded but opened up so you can get a sense of the land. Sites 1 through 6 are prime real estate by the creek—but the rest, on the other side of the road, offer privacy. The drinking water is cold and clean. Chester, with all the supplies a body could ever require, is a hop, skip, and a jump down the bucolic country road past little farms, old orchards, and rough little vacation homes. Good hikes splay out from the campground to just about everywhere. Or you can get in your car and explore Lassen Volcanic National Park, the most underused national park in the West.

Read the Warner Valley Campground register to see how revered this place is: "Always come here, always will." "Dave's twentieth summer here." "Beautiful place to make a baby." "Trails are the best." "Lovely, quiet, serene." "Great swimming in Hot Springs Creek." "God's country." "Perfecto mundo." "Absolutely divine!" "Don't tell anyone about this place."

CAMPGROUND RATINGS

Beauty:	★★★★★
Site privacy:	★★★★★
Site spaciousness:	★★★★★
Quiet:	★★★★
Security:	★★★★★
Cleanliness/upkeep:	★★★★

Read the camp register and become a believer. This campground is a jewel to cherish.

The only fly in the ointment is the fishing. Fishing is not great in Lassen Volcanic National Park. Since the mid-1970s the Park Service has not stocked most of the park's lakes and streams. However, near Warner Valley Campground, just outside the park, is some fine fishing. Try the Caribou Wilderness to the east—hike into the lakes. Caribou, Echo, and Silver Lakes are well stocked, but folks can drive to them, so they get heavy play. To the south are Lake Almanor and Deer Creek, both of which have great fishing.

Okay, so you can't live off the land at Warner Valley Campground. The only local food supply in the immediate area is the cook house at the Drakesbad Guest Ranch by the campground. They provide a *Brotzeit* (hiker's plate) to anybody who arrives at the cook shack clutching $6.95. For this you get a hungry-hiker trail kit containing selected slices of meat, cheese, and wine, beer, or soda.

Rooms at the resort run about $100 per person per night for three hots and a cot and a chair by the geothermally heated pool. Horseback riding on the resort herd is extra. Still, Drakesbad Guest Ranch is legendary and should be on the agenda of a "do everything" California explorer at least once in a lifetime. The place (settled by a relative of both Sir Francis Drake and the more contemporary Jim Drake of Santa Monica, inventor of the Windsurfer) is almost a century old. People come here the same week in summer year after year. So reserve ahead at (916) 529-1512 for the brochure, or phone the long-distance operator and ask for the Drakesbad Toll Station #2 through Susanville, California, in the summer.

A good little hike from Warner Valley Campground is up to Boiling Springs Lake. The trailhead is on the left, a few hundred yards past the campground on the way to the visible Drakesbad Resort. Follow the obvious trail and cross Hot Springs Creek on the bridge. Reach a junction. A right takes you to Drakesbad Lake, Dream Lake, and Devils Kitchen. Go left and reach another junction where the trail to the right goes to Drake Lake and, again, Devils Kitchen (another must-do hike, with fumaroles and mud pots). Follow the signs and you will smell and hear Boiling Springs Lake before you arrive. The rotten-egg smell is the hydrogen sulfide from sulfur in the rising gases. The "bumping" is from the mud pots, which open and close like some monstrous earthen eye. Here's a hell even an atheist can believe in. The water is hot and yellow and green. Green from some algae, and yellow from opal and iron oxide. It is hot enough to scald and kill you. Stay on the trail. You can fall through the thin crust and land in an incipient mud pot.

Last time I was at Warner Valley Campground was in September, and we had the place to ourselves. I swam in the pool just below the wooden bridge crossing Hot Springs Creek at the beginning of the Boiling Springs Lake Trail. Other times, when the campground was busier, we went downstream and found great pools off the road below the Ranger Station.

Weather here can be dicey. Come prepared for both extremes, and be sure to phone ahead in early summer to make sure the campground is open. The Lassen area is notorious for being snowed in through early summer.

KEY INFORMATION

Warner Valley Campground, Lassen Volcanic National Park

Superintendent
P.O Box 100
Mineral, CA 96063-0100

Operated by: National Park Service

Information: (530) 595-4444; www.nps.gov/lavo

Open: Mid-June through early October (depending on road and weather conditions)

Individual sites: 18 sites for tents or small RVs; 2 group sites, reservation only

Each site has: Picnic table, fire ring, bear box

Registration: At entrance

Facilities: Water, pit toilets

Parking: At individual site

Fee: $12

Elevation: 5,650 feet

Restrictions:

Pets—On leash only

Fires—In fire ring

Vehicles—No trailers, no large RVs

Other—Don't leave food out; use bear boxes

To get there: from Chester on Highway 36, turn onto Warner Valley Road by the fire station. Bear left at the first junction (0.6 mile), and bear right at the next junction (5.5 miles). Drive 9.9 miles into the park and to Warner Valley Campground. (You will pass Warner Valley Ranger Station on the way.

NORTHERN CALIFORNIA

SIERRA NEVADA

SIERRA NEVADA

BLUE LAKES CAMPGROUNDS

Eldorado National Forest, near Carson Pass

Head up Blue Lakes Road near Carson Pass, but make certain you have all your ice and supplies, because it is a long way back to town. The nearest shopping is at Woodfords, or up over the pass and down at Caples Lake—but they don't have much. For the first 7 miles off CA 88 (Carson Pass National Scenic Byway) you breeze along the nicely paved Blue Lakes Road by the West Fork Carson River. Then the road turns to dirt for the last bone-jarring 5 miles to Lower Blue Lake. This poor old road gets washed out every spring, and the county has to go in and blade it up again. You pass lots of dusty guys in old-style Jeeps looking happy (there's some good off-road driving on Deer Valley Jeep Road, which cuts through the Mokolumne Wilderness to the Ebbetts Pass Road, and on the Summit City Road, which goes through to Red Lake on CA 88). All the scenery is spectacular. Then you come through the dust and pines and see the Blue Lakes.

The Blue Lakes have everything but motorboats: trout, granite islands you can swim to, wildflowered meadows, rugged granite ridges, and clear-blue water cold enough to ice down a six-pack. This is heaven.

I ogled Lower Blue Lake Campground and Middle Creek Campground, then inspected Upper Blue Lake Dam Campground, above the dam, before finally

CAMPGROUND RATINGS

Beauty:	★★★★★
Site privacy:	★★★★★
Site spaciousness:	★★★★★
Quiet:	★★★★★
Security:	★★★★★
Cleanliness/upkeep:	★★★★

Come to Blue Lakes with a week's worth of ice and supplies because you won't want to go home.

deciding to set up camp at Upper Blue Lake Campground. Why? I don't like to camp below a dam. This is earthquake country.

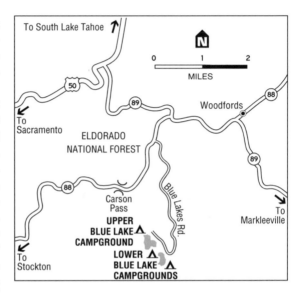

One day in March 1872, at 2:30 A.M., a monster hit the Owens Valley. Felt as far east as Salt Lake City, as far north as Canada, and as far south as Mexico, it shook old John Muir over in Yosemite Valley. He wrote: "I was awakened by a tremendous earthquake, and though I had never enjoyed a storm of this sort, the strange thrilling motion could not be mistaken, and I ran out of the cabin, both glad and frightened, shouting, 'A noble earthquake! A noble earthquake!' feeling sure I was going to learn something."

I want to learn something, but I don't want to get wet. And, fortunately, both Upper Blue Lake Dam Campground and Upper Blue Lake Campground allay all the worries of the earthquake-conscious camper. Previously, we camped up at Upper Blue Lake Campground, figuring the campground farthest from the dam is bound to be better. I think it still is, but recently Pacific Gas & Electric, which operates the camp, replaced the water system and had to cut a few trees and reditch for the plumbing.

I asked the hostess who came around for the campground fee where the good hiking trails were. She gave me "Bob's Hiking Map," which was a many-times Xeroxed godsend showing one where to expect the nude bathers, where to find all the little lakes, where to locate all the old trails, and where to find all the flowers. My family found flowers. There is a meadow just around the northwest side of Upper Blue Lake that was in spectacular bloom. We saw lupines, bachelor's buttons, forget-me-nots, shooting stars, buttercups, yellow snap dragons, swamp lilies, little pink button flowers, Virginia bluebells, penstamen, mule ears, fireweed, and more.

By the campground, the water is shallow and good for swimming. I hiked down through the dwarf mountain willow (deciduous and growing all over the place) and walked out into the water far enough to swim. Remember to bring shoes for wading. Great fun would be a cheap inflatable boat to loll about in, arm flung overboard, face to the warm sun.

People were pulling up fish all over the place. The best luck on Upper Blue was above the dam—from the shore. I saw people trolling the deep waters of Lower Blue where Middle Creek runs down from the dam. I heard somebody bragging about his catch up at Grouse Lake. A path heads to Grouse from a trailhead below Upper Blue Lake Dam.

It is also possible to access the Pacific Crest Trail. On your way in from CA 88, you will pass the trailhead before you get to Lower Blue Lake. You can go either way, although I hear the climb up toward Carson Pass is a bear. You also can access the trail by hiking up the Summit City Road above Upper Blue Lake Campground. Look for a Jeep trail on the right that will take you up a ridge to Lost Lakes and the Pacific Crest Trail.

I loved Upper Blue Lake Campground. The pit toilets were immaculate. They even had the paper toilet covers, which pleased my hygiene-conscious sister.

To get there: from Woodfords, take Highway 88 west and turn left on Blue Lakes Road. Continue 12 miles (the last 5 miles are on a dirt road). First you will see Lower Blue Lake Campground, then Middle Creek, Upper Blue Lake Dam, and Upper Blue Lake Campgrounds respectively.

KEY INFORMATION

Blue Lakes Campgrounds
Eldorado National Forest
3070 Camino Heights Drive
Camino, CA 95709
or

PG&E Land Projects
P.O. Box 277444
Sacramento, CA 95827

Operated by: U.S. Forest Service

Information: (916) 386-5164 (Eldorado), (415) 973-5552 (Pacific Gas & Electric); www.hwy88camping.com

Open: End of May through September (depending on road and weather conditions)

Individual sites: Upper Blue Lake has 32 sites; Upper Blue Lake Dam has 25; Lower Blue Lake has 16

Each site has: Picnic table, fireplace

Registration: At entrance

Facilities: Water every third site, vault toilets

Parking: At individual site

Fee: $13; add. charge for extra vehicles or pets

Elevation: 8,200 feet

Restrictions:

Pets—On leash only

Fires—In fireplace

Vehicles—RVs and trailers up to 34 feet (difficult road)

Other—Don't leave food out

BUCKEYE CAMPGROUND

Toiyabe National Forest, near Bridgeport

All roads that lead to Buckeye Campground also pass the Burger Barn in Bridgeport. Anytime is a good time for an everything-on-it burger, wrapped in wax paper, at the outside tables of this ageless monument to roadside dining. Historic Bridgeport's Burger Barn is a famous relic of Americana. One assumes that the lean, tasty burger meat comes from close relatives of the sleek cattle grazing in the knee-deep grass around town. After all, this is cattle country. In Bridgeport, the heart of the Old West steadily beats.

There are four loops to the campground. The first loop you come to on the left, sites 42 through 68, has flush toilets and the campground host (employed by L & L Inc. concessionaires). Bundles of wood are sold at the host station. You continue up the hill for the other three loops. Two have pit toilets, and the other has flush toilets but was closed the last time I was up there .

At 7,000 feet, Buckeye is Big Country camping. The air smells of pine, dust, and cold rushing water. Buckeye Creek runs right past the campground. The mountain wildflowers grow from the sandy needled floor among the sage. You look up and see the rocky slopes and, farther on, the white of the glaciers on the peaks: cowboy country. A horse trail cuts right by the camp. The sites are mostly unoccupied; the pitches are scoured clean by the winter. This is an excellent place to camp.

CAMPGROUND RATINGS

Beauty:	★★★★★
Site privacy:	★★★★★
Site spaciousness:	★★★★★
Quiet:	★★★★★
Security:	★★★★★
Cleanliness/upkeep:	★★★★★

Buckeye Campground is a place of pine and sage and cold rushing water. Come for fishing, hiking, and the magnificent rocky slopes and far-off glaciers.

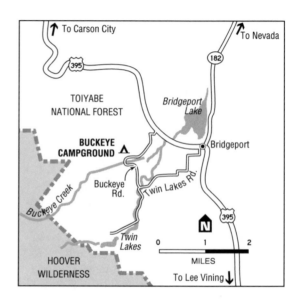

Fishing is not bad on Buckeye Creek between the two bridges—that's where the fish are stocked. You can hie on over to Twin Lakes and rent a boat. Go for the big brown trout. In 1987 somebody caught the state record, a 26.5 pounder, here. However, most of the folks I saw with fish had little rainbows. The water-skiing on Upper Twin scares away some of the trout, so the best fishing is on Lower Twin. I talked with one old-timer who said the best time to come for the browns is in May, when it is cold and windy. Troll with Rapelas, he advised. I threw in some salmon eggs and didn't get a nibble.

Another big draw at Buckeye Campground is the hot springs. They are by the stream down from the campground. It's best to get in your car and drive down the hill. Take your first left and climb a slight hill. There is a slanting parking area immediately on the right. Climb down the steep slope to the hot pools by the river below. This can be fun. Wear shoes with some bite since the footing is slippery. Sometimes the pools are empty, sometimes filled with fun-loving folks. Last time I was there, one pool was occupied by a lone, naked, whalelike chap who looked to me boiled-lobster pink. I chose to wear bathing apparel. I sat in the hot (nonstinky) pool, then sat in Buckeye Creek to cool off.

Good hiking can be had right out of camp. Buckeye Campground is in a **V** between the two branches of Buckeye Creek. The two hikes follow the two branches upstream and ultimately swing around and join one another, so you can make up to a 16-mile loop. Bring fishing gear since there are elusive brown trout and rainbow in the upper reaches; use local worms and try the pools behind beaver dams. The trailhead to the two hikes is up above the campground loops. Just walk up the access road (newly tarred and graveled) and it will dead-end into a horse corral and the trailhead (map posted there).

One trail heads west up along the right-hand branch of Buckeye Creek. This trail follows an erstwhile wagon road up through flowered meadows and pine forest. The trail up the left-hand branch of Buckeye Creek can be accessed from the campground's left-hand loops (looking west). Just walk to the creek and head up the fisherman's trail. Otherwise, walk from the trailhead a few hundred yards until the trail winds left up a ridge to the stream. The wildflowers in July were all over the place—lupine, shooting star, paintbrush. Watch the campground notice board for ranger wildflower nature walks—they are fun.

Bring ice—the nearest supplies are at Doc and Al's, or Bridgeport. Think about cooling your beer and sodas in the stream. Or buy a cheap Styrofoam cooler, fill it with ice, duct-tape it shut, and put it in a cool place for ice refill. Mind the bears. Put all your food stuff in the car trunk when you go off. Bears are busy tending their cubs and looking for chow during camping season. By fall, bears max out, eating 20,000 calories every day in preparation for hibernation.

Good side trips from Buckeye are to Bodie (bring food and water), Mono Lake, and the Virginia Creek Settlement (once part of Dogtown, a gold-rush mining camp) for a look around and a meal. Go gem hunting near Bridgeport. Head 3.3 miles north from Bridgeport on CA 182, and turn right on Forest Service Road 046. Head out exploring (avoid any active mines) for quartz crystals, chalcopyrite, and pyrite.

KEY INFORMATION

Buckeye Campground, Humboldt–Toiyabe National Forest Bridgeport Ranger Station HCR 1 Box 1000 Bridgeport, CA 93517-0595

Operated by: U.S. Forest Service

Information: (760) 932-7070; www.fs.fed.us/htnf

Open: May through October (depending on road and weather conditions)

Individual sites: 65 sites

Each site has: Picnic table, fire ring

Registration: At entrance to each loop

Facilities: Water, flush and vault toilets, drinking water

Parking: At individual site

Fee: $9

Elevation: 7,500 feet

Restrictions:

Pets—On leash only

Fires—In fire ring

Vehicles—RVs up to 30 feet

Other—Don't leave food out

To get there: from Bridgeport, take the Twin Lakes Road southwest to Buckeye Road on the right by Doc and Al's Resort. Go 4 miles on the dirt road to the campground.

CHUTE HILL CAMPGROUND

Malakoff Diggins State Historical Park, near Nevada City

Chute Hill Campground is set on the hill above Malakoff Diggins and North Bloomfield—the Diggins was an awesome hydraulic mining operation, and North Bloomfield is the town that served it. The campground is excellent. All the sites are set in under huge old ponderosa pines along a meandering access road. Those sites down below are on the rim overlooking the Diggins and the town. There are some flush toilets (which gets an A+ from my schoolteacher wife), some vaults, and peculiar fire pits made out of steel drums that were difficult to light— use lots of tinder to get a draft going. Although Chute Hill Campground is on a kind of bench, all of the campsites seemed to run a few degrees downhill, which is just fine for tents, but I saw folks with small campers struggling to get their sleeping vehicle level enough for a good snooze.

Just down the road, or down the Slaughterhouse Trail or North Bloomfield Trail (both accessible from the campground), is North Bloomfield, which has a drugstore, one saloon, a general store, post office, blacksmith shop, fire station, and so forth. Today North Bloomfield is peaceful, but that was not always the case. In its day, the town was humming. There were seven saloons and two breweries. The infamous E. Clampus Vitus Drinking Society (wild but decent folks) had a meeting hall here.

CAMPGROUND RATINGS

Beauty: ★★★★★
Site privacy: ★★★★
Site spaciousness: ★★★★
Quiet: ★★★★
Security: ★★★★★
Cleanliness/upkeep: ★★★★

Chute Campground is an excellent campground next to the eerie Diggins and historic North Bloomfield. Feel the ghosts of the forty-niners.

In their heyday, under their flag depicting a hoop skirt with their motto, "This is the flag we fight under," singing "We'll Take a Drink with Thee, Dear Brother," the Clampus fraternity raised some hell. And North Bloomfield wasn't so prissy, either. As one visitor put it: "The streets are half a leg deep in filth and mud, rendering getting about awful beyond description. The city is one great cesspool of mud, offal, garbage, dead animals and that worst of nuisances consequent upon the entire absence of outhouses."

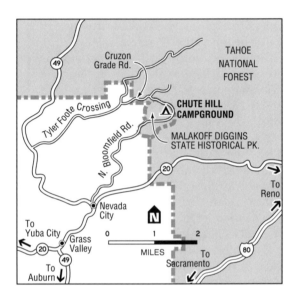

Now, get to the Diggins. There's a monstrous beauty here: the washed-away mountain like a miniature Grand Canyon, with rust-tipped white formations resembling minarets and towers all touched with green pine. A century ago, this was environmental hell. Miners brought water down from the High Country via flumes and ran it through a huge leather hose connected to nozzles known as monitors to wash down entire mountains. The runoff was filtered through sluice boxes in search of gold. It was ungodly. Everything downstream was destroyed. Even the cattle wouldn't drink the runoff. Not until 1884 did a farmer named Woodruff sue the North Bloomfield Gravel and Mining Company and win. The days of "hydraulicking" whole mountains were over. Mining companies had to respect their neighbors' property. They say $10 billion of gold remains in the Blue Lead—the ancient river the miners were washing out. The Diggins remains as an eerie monument to man's greed and ingenuity.

Hike the Rim Trail that circles the Diggins. Then hike the Diggins Loop Trail. Come prepared for Hiller Tunnel. Bring flashlights, a hat, and shoes that won't slip on wet rock. Hiller Tunnel was part of all the ditches, tunnels, flumes, and reservoirs that supplied water to the Diggins—just one drainage tunnel was 7,800 feet long. Imagine the amount of disciplined labor it took to run Malakoff Diggins. In fact, hydraulic mining was the deathknell of the classic forty-niner who wandered all over the Sierra with a pick, pan, rifle, and mule. From then on, miners became wage slaves, building projects like Hiller Tunnel, which is fun for us to explore when the weather is dry but a beating when it rains.

Remember to buy all your provisions in Grass Valley on the way in. Nevada City has some markets, but they are hard to park by. Most of the supermarkets are in Grass Valley. There is a nice corner store on Tyler Foot Crossing Road where Oak Tree Road and Purdon Road cross. This store is a natural food store, so don't expect to find Polish sausage or any other meats for that matter. They do have wonderful local produce, however, as well as beer and ice.

The other road in, the North Bloomfield Road, is a little rough by the park. After a rain it gets hairy. And by the South Yuba River, the road negotiates the world's steepest hill. It's best to go into Malakoff Diggins State Historical Park via Tyler Foot Crossing Road and come out via the North Bloomfield Road, on the general philosophy that going down on a bad road is better than going up.

To get there: from Nevada City, head north 10.4 miles on Highway 49. Turn right on Tyler Foote Crossing Road and drive 12.2 miles. Turn right on Cruzon Grade Road and follow the signs. Chute Hill Campground will be on your right before you reach North Bloomfield and Park Headquarters.

KEY INFORMATION

Chute Hill Campground Malakoff Diggins State Historical Park
23579 North Bloomfield Road Nevada City, CA 95959

Operated by: California Department of Parks and Recreation

Information: (530) 265-2740; http://parks.ca.gov

Open: April through November

Individual sites: 30 sites for tents or RVs, 3 rustic cabins

Each site has: Picnic table, fire pit

Registration: By entrance; reserve by phone, (800) 444-7275, or online, www.reserveamerica.com

Facilities: Water, running water in cabins in the summer, flush and pit toilets, wood for sale

Parking: At individual site

Fee: $10 camping site or rustic cabin; $8.65 nonrefundable reservation fee

Elevation: 3,500 feet

Restrictions:

Pets—On leash only

Fires—In fire pit

Vehicles—RVs up to 24 feet, trailers up to 18 feet

Other—Reservations on holidays and summer weekends recommended

D. L. BLISS STATE PARK

Lake Tahoe, near Meeks Bay

L ake Tahoe, the queen of California lakes, faces a mountain of woes—population and pollution threaten the lake's natural beauty—but if you come to D. L. Bliss State Park and hike down the Rubicon Trail toward Emerald Bay State Park, you'll see Tahoe almost as Mark Twain did. He wrote, "The air up there is very pure and fine, bracing and delicious. It is the same air the angels breathe. . . . The view was always fascinating, bewitching, entrancing." Tahoe still has the same effect, and D. L. Bliss State Park shows her off at her best.

Who was D. L. Bliss? Finding the answer took a bit of research. Finally, I tracked down Mr. Duane LeRoy Bliss. No nature lover, he was a ruthless lumberman who made a fortune cutting down most of the trees in the Tahoe Basin. After his demise, an heir guiltily donated some of the denuded acres to the State of California.

Now, besides being reforested and magically beautiful, D. L. Bliss State Park is a parent's delight. The place is crawling with kids playing under the pines and climbing the rounded boulders in the campground. We brought our big-city niece to Bliss, and within moments she was running around the campground playing hide-and-seek with all the kids. And the flush toilets are immaculately clean and the hot showers are heavenly after a day of swimming down at Lester Beach (the best beach in Tahoe for kids)

CAMPGROUND RATINGS

Beauty:	★★★★★
Site privacy:	★★★
Site spaciousness:	★★★★
Quiet:	★★★
Security:	★★★★★
Cleanliness/upkeep:	★★★★★

Come armed with reservations, kids, water gear, camera, and hiking boots—this is high-profile California camping.

and hiking the Rubicon Trail to Emerald Bay and back.

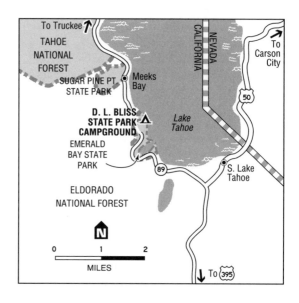

There are three campground areas. One area, campsites 141 through 168, is close to Lester Beach. These sites must be reserved. You must specifically request them and they cost an extra $5 per night. The sites are packed in—tents only—and a little sandy, so it's not a bad idea to bring a tarp or strip of AstroTurf to put in front of your tent, or better still, a basin to fill with water so the kiddies can dip their feet before dragging sand into the tent, and ultimately into your sleeping bag.

The next group of campsites, sites 91 through 140, are a half-mile from Lester Beach. These sites are more spread out, but still heavily used. I like camping still farther up the hill at sites 1 through 90 (site 22 is great!), where it is roomier and the ground is covered with a bed of pine needles. You are a mile from the beach but you can walk or drive (folks camping can always park below even if the day use parking lot is full). This is kid-o-rama as well and has the advantage of not being on the main drag.

On the beach the sand is white and clean and perfect for making sand castles. This is good news since the water is freezing and fit only for walruses or Nordic rites of manhood. A couple handy items here are one of those cheap little blow-up boats and an electric pump that plugs into the car's cigarette lighter. With this outfit, you can float around the buoyed-off swimming area and read a novel. Or the kids can splash in and out of it and dump each other into the gelid water. There are no lifeguards, but people keep a pretty close eye on their kids and everyone else's.

Fishing at Lake Tahoe is either really great (when you score) or a total shutout. The clear, beautiful water is the problem. Fish need algae to support a food chain. Still, mackinaw trout, rainbow trout, and kokanee salmon can be found. They tend to stay at low depths in areas that provide them some cover—find mackinaws near Emerald Bay, in the northwest, and off the south shore. Rainbows lurk anywhere there's a rocky bottom. Nobody seemed to know where kokanee salmon hide. They just show up, and if you happen to be there—eureka! Everyone agrees the fishing is best in the early morning and evening and on cloudy days.

The biking in D. L. Bliss State Park is poor since the park is on a fairly steep hill. Still, there is good biking around Lake Tahoe. One paved bike path leads to the Truckee River, a good ways down the northeast shore of the lake. Another begins below Emerald Bay State Park and curls around the south shore.

Hiking the Rubicon Trail is a must. You can access the trail (stop at the Visitor Center for a map) just south of Lester Beach or from a parking area just below the check-in station. Just cross the road and you'll see the sign for the trail.

Avoid Lake Tahoe's southeast corner unless you can bear 8 miles of motels and restaurants with outdoors-sounding names. Highway 89 from the north or south is much friendlier. Shop in Tahoe City near the north end of the lake. A little store at Meeks Bay offers ice, beer, and sundries.

To get there: from the intersection of Highway 89 and U.S. 50 in South Lake Tahoe, drive 11 miles north on Highway 89 past the entrance to Emerald Bay State Park, to the D. L. Bliss State Park entrance on the right. Meeks Bay is a few miles north of the park entrance.

KEY INFORMATION

D. L. Bliss State Park
P.O. Box 266
Tahoma, CA 95733

Operated by: California Department of Parks and Recreation

Information: (530) 525-7277, (760) 765-0755 (Park H.Q.); http://parks.ca.gov

Open: May through October

Individual sites: 168 sites for tents or RVs under 16 feet

Each site has: Picnic table, fireplace

Registration: 1 mile past entrance; reserve by phone, (800) 444-7275, or online, www.reserveamerica.com

Facilities: Water, flush toilets, showers, wood for sale

Parking: At individual site

Fee: $12 ; $8.65 nonrefundable reservation fee

Elevation: 6,920 feet

Restrictions:

Pets—On leash only; $1 fee

Fires—In fireplace

Vehicles—RVs up to 16 feet

Other—Reservations on holidays and summer weekends required; 8 person maximum; can only get Fridays and Saturdays by reservations

SIERRA NEVADA

GROVER HOT SPRINGS STATE PARK

Grover Hot Springs State Park, near Markleeville

First off—Quaking Aspen Campground and Toiyabe Campground are just different loops in one campground in Grover Hot Springs State Park. Secondly, it is a family park. "Oh, my gosh!" the nice lady ranger exclaimed, taking a sideways look at my grizzled visage. "You don't want to be here in the summer when school's out. This place is full of kids!"

Well, if you have kids, Grover Hot Springs (named after Alvin M. Grover, one of the original Anglo owners) is the place to be. There are lots of other kids to play with your kids so you can kick back for a change. There's a nice warm swimming pool watched over by healthy, young lifeguards; a nonthreatening stream full of fish and other interesting denizens; miles of trails up rounded hills; miles of nontrafficked roads to bike on. grassy meadows; a nearby western town with a museum, supplies, and horse rentals; a nature trail; hot showers; flush toilets; and a big, uncrowded camp to run around like a wild animal.

The corollary to all the summer activity is that you must RESERVE, RESERVE, RESERVE! Make sure you have a campsite before dragging your kids all the way up here to find the place jammed. Some of the campsites here are by Hot Springs Creek. At first that might seem enviable, but this is where the fishermen fish and the excited kids play in the stream. Better to reserve a site off the creek, backed into the woods.

CAMPGROUND RATINGS

Beauty:	★★★★
Site privacy:	★★★
Site spaciousness:	★★★★
Quiet:	★★★
Security:	★★★★★
Cleanliness/upkeep:	★★★★

Great for kids in the summer, good adult camping the rest of the year. Hot springs. Magnificent vistas—this is Big Country.

Stay away from the bathrooms as well.

During the rest of the year, Grover Hot Springs is wide open for killjoy geezers who don't thrill to the trill of youthful voices. This is a beautiful park. It's well run and clean. The hike up to the waterfall is just enough to get the blood pumping but not stress the pacemaker. The hot springs bath adjacent to the pool is guarateed rejuvenation with lingering powers.

The hot spring doesn't smell. Somehow, the waters

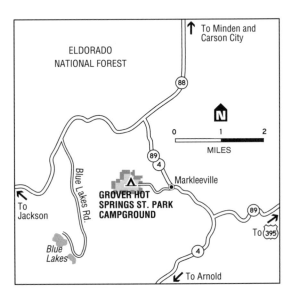

issue forth from the earth without that rotten-egg sulfur smell. When the Sierra Nevada rose as one huge chunk millions of years ago, the violent changes caused faulting, that is, cracks in the massive rock structure. Water from the surface, then, works it way down through the faults to the magma where the rock is hot as hell, then boils back to the surface as hot spring waters replete with minerals it has dissolved along its way. The minerals include sodium chloride, sodium sulfate, sodium carbonate; calcium carbonate; magnesium carbonate; and a little iron, alumina, and silica. This means lots of salt. I definitely felt better after my cure. The water is hot, about 103°F; that's cooler than the 148°F that it was when it left the ground. The hot pool is right next to the swimming pool.

There are good hikes around the camp. Find campsites 35 and 36, and you'll be at the extra vehicle parking lot where a marked trail heads west for the waterfall. It heads along beautiful meadows and through pine woods—mostly Jeffrey pines. Stick your nose right up to the bark and sniff. The Jeffrey pine smells just like vanilla. Another salient fact that I learned from the *Grover Hot*

Springs State Park Guide to the Park's Transitional Walk concerns the Jeffrey pine's cones, which are primary food for the reddish-black Douglas squirrel. The guide asserts that "of the millions of seeds produced during the lifetime of a pine tree only one, on the average, will grow into a new tree!"

On the trail to the falls, you cross some seeps and soon enough hear the falls. When the water is low, you can go up beside the streambed to the falls. In spring, however, count on climbing up the rocks just ahead of you to approach the falls. The round-trip should take you a little more than an hour.

Nearby Markleeville, population 100, is worth a trip. Visit the museum at the Alpine County Historical Complex. In 1861 Bactrain camels from Mongolia were brought here to be used as pack animals. Bad move. Conditions in the Gobi desert are a lot different from those in the Sierra Nevada. However, modern packers have made good use of the Peruvian llama, a cousin of the camel obviously better bred for life on the Pacific Rim.

Another fun cultural trip is to Genoa for the Mormon Station Historical State Monument. This little park with its stockade, museum, and picnic facilities used to be a relief station for travelling pioneers. Basically, the tired travelers staggered into the station and were promptly overcharged for their bed, bath, and meal. Most men arrived on horseback and left on shank's mare. The owners of the station fattened up the horses and sold them back to new travelers with more cash. Right across the street was and is the oldest tavern in Nevada, where the fleeced traveler could drown his sorrows.

KEY INFORMATION

Grover Hot Springs State Park
P.O. Box 188
Markleeville, CA 96120

Operated by: California Department of Parks and Recreation

Information: (530) 694-2248; http://parks.ca.gov

Open: All year

Individual sites: 26 sites for tents only, 13 sites for RVs, 37 sites for tents or RVs up to 27 feet

Each site has: Picnic table, fireplace, bear box, water faucet every 3 sites

Registration: By entrance; reserve by phone, (800) 444-7275, or online, www.reserveamerica.com

Facilities: Water, flush toilets, showers (except in the winter), wood for sale

Parking: At individual site

Fee: $12; $8.65 nonrefundable reservation fee

Elevation: 6,000 feet

Restrictions:

Pets—On leash only

Fires—In fireplace

Vehicles—RVs up to 27 feet, trailers up to 24 feet

Other—Reservations on holidays and summer recommended

To get there: from Markleeville, head about 4 miles west on Hot Springs Road.

SIERRA NEVADA

HASKINS VALLEY CAMPGROUND

Bucks Lake, near Quincy

Here's another beautiful campground in Pacific Gas & Electric (PG&E) land. As usual, the campground is well conceived and well tended. PG&E is mindful of its image and sets out to curry favor with the public, ever apprehensive of its problems when it sometimes has to draw down the level of its reservoirs in late summer to satisfy us energy guzzlers in the flatland below. That's when folks look around and say, "Hey, Bucks Lake isn't a lake at all, but a reservoir contained by a dam. And Haskins Valley is named for the valley where the lake is now."

Still, I love Bucks Lake, Haskins Valley Campground, and electric lights, all in that order. The sites are set on a handsome pined knoll embraced by the lake. All you see is the waving green of the pines and the sparkling blue-green sky and water. What a spot to spend a week! This is kick back and relax country. Quincy is just down the way, so you don't have to worry about serious supplies. There is a store right on the lake that sells sundries. In Meadow Valley below the road splits to make a low road and a high road to Bucks Lake. Take the 2-mile-longer low option, Big Creek Road, if you don't trust your ancient flivver (and admire incredible dogwoods). At Bucks Lake, you'll find boats to rent, shoreline to explore, hikes to take, and a lake that warms up in summer to temperatures that suit the most spoiled swimmer.

CAMPGROUND RATINGS

Beauty: ★★★★★
Site privacy: ★★★
Site spaciousness: ★★★
Quiet: ★★★
Security: ★★★
Cleanliness/upkeep: ★★★★

This is easy summer camping, with lazy afternoons of reading novels and fishing the lake. Nearby Quincy is a good visit.

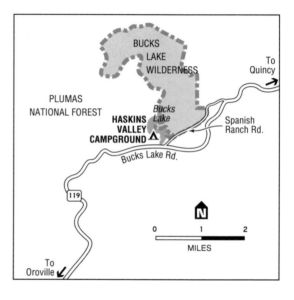

Think summer camping. Bring a tent you can stand up in—sit in your folding chair. Think about a screen house. There are voracious mosquitoes in this area. Out there when the bloodsuckers are buzzing in your ears, a screen house is worth its weight in gold. The last time I was out at Bucks Lake, I complained about the mosquitoes and heard the polite laughter of an elderly couple a campsite away who were sitting genteelly in their screen house around a card table. I found Coleman sold a minimal version, and I bought it. Now I'm looking forward to sitting in it, reading a novel, and listening to unenlightened campers slapping skeeters.

Bucks Lake is heavy-duty cross-country skiing territory. In fact, this area, notably Johnsville, takes credit for introducing the sport of skiing to the West. Apparently, miners from Norway and Sweden built "long boards" or "snow-shoes" from planks up to 12 feet long, weighing about 20 pounds. Now we call them skis. The miners used them to get around in deep snow—for fun, they started downhill races above Eureka Lake. According to legend, they reached up to 80 mph; a long ski pole held between the legs was used as a brake or as a pivot around which to turn.

Quincy is a fun visit. Looking like a movie set for the all-American town, Quincy is the Plumas County seat and home to the Plumas County Museum, which chronicles Quincy's involvement with gold mining, logging, and the railroad. Imagine the wives arriving from the East to join their gold-miner husbands at Quincy. One wrote, "Our fare is very plain, consisting of meat and bread, bread and meat, now and then some rancid butter that was put up in the Land Of Goshen [the East] and sent on a six-month cruise by Cape Horn, for which we give the sum of $2 a pound." Of course, all this on top of crude log cabins, rowdy forty-niners, and the heartbreak of betting your all on striking it rich.

The museum also has a decent exhibit on the Maidu Indians, the previous leaseholders of the area that includes Plumas County (named for bird feathers a Spanish explorer observed in the river). The Maidu, who ironically never valued gold, did use gold-laced quartz for spear tips, knives, and mortars. They were low-key Native Americans who "trod very lightly" on the land and at first gazed with curiosity at the forty-niners and their industrious ways. For a while, the Maidu were happy to find gold to trade with the white man for a shirt or a pair of pantaloons. Soon enough, however, the two groups collided and the Maidu passed rapidly into history.

When you drive around Quincy, look at the trees—the impressive oak, maple, and poplar. Quincy folks were loggers and they knew their trees. Look for the Morning Thunder Cafe—good breakfasts. Then drive up Bucks Lake Road—11 miles to the Bucks Summit Trailhead—and climb your calories off ascending the southern flank of Mount Pleasant.

KEY INFORMATION

Haskins Valley Campground
PG&E Land Projects
P.O. Box 277444
Sacramento, CA 95827

Operated by: Pacific Gas & Electric

Information: (916) 386-5164

Open: May 21 to October 15 (depending on road and weather conditions)

Individual sites: 65 sites for tents or RVs

Each site has: Picnic table, fireplace, barbecue

Registration: At entrance

Facilities: Water, vault toilets

Parking: At individual site

Fee: $15

Elevation: 5,200 feet

Restrictions:

Pets—On leash only

Fires—In fireplace

Vehicles—RVs and trailers allowed (no hookups)

Other—Don't leave food out

To get there: from Quincy, turn west on Bucks Lake Road, and drive 16.5 miles to the campground.

SIERRA NEVADA

OAK HOLLOW CAMPGROUND

Calaveras Big Trees State Park, near Arnold

In 1852 hungry miners needed red meat. And that was what Augustus T. Dowd was after one fine spring day as he chased a wounded bear up the Stanislaus River. Intead he found some of the biggest trees he'd ever seen. Using a string, he measured one of the trees. When he got back to town, the string was found to be over 100 feet long. The story is, nobody believed Augustus T. Dowd and nobody would go with him to see the leviathan trees. Later, Dowd told everybody he had shot a huge bear, and when curious folks straggled after him to see the bear they saw the Big Tree instead. Pointing to the immense trunk and lofty top, Dowd cried out, "Boys, do you now believe my big tree story? This is the large grizzly bear I wanted you to see. Do you still think it's a yarn?"

Indeed, the Big Tree is an awesome sight. John Muir noted, "The Big Tree is nature's forest masterpiece, and as far as I know, the greatest of living things. It belongs to an ancient stock, as its remains in old rocks show, and has a strange air of other days about it, a thoroughbred look inherited from the long ago—the auld lang syne of trees."

Hardly had the forty-niners' wonder faded when they resolved to cut a Big Tree down. They tried axes and saws. Nothing doing. Finally they took to drilling by pump augurs through to the center from opposite sides. It took five men 22 days to

CAMPGROUND RATINGS

Beauty:	★★★★
Site privacy:	★★★
Site spaciousness:	★★★★
Quiet:	★★★
Security:	★★★★★
Cleanliness/upkeep:	★★★★★

Open all year, the best camping at Calaveras Big Trees State Park is fall through spring. Don't forget to stop at Columbia State Historical Park.

accomplish the job. The tree fell with a crash heard from miles around. Immediately the bark was stripped off and sent to New York City to show the folks the wonders of California. And soon, folks came to the Big Trees.

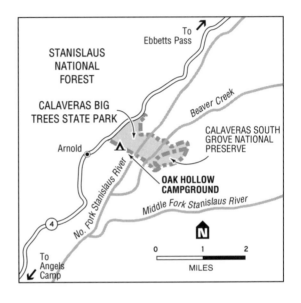

They danced on dance floors made from the stumps. They rode horses through hollowed out Big Tree logs. They bowled on alleys made from the trees. They named the giants fancifully, as in "Pride of the Forest," or after heroes, such as "Washington." They argued over what to call the Big Tree—"Vegetable Monster" was one name in vogue briefly. But sequoia seems to have won out (sequoia after a Cherokee Indian, Sequoyah, who established an alphabet for the Cherokee language). Then they named the Big Tree Grove "Calaveras" after a skull found in some caves nearby—the skull was probably from an Indian burial.

Now we can camp under the Calaveras Big Trees at North Grove Campground—although the camping is lots better down at nearby Oak Hollow Campground. Never mind that Oak Hollow Campground has no Big Trees. It's a beautiful campground and a good base camp to explore the Calaveras South Grove Natural Preserve. At South Grove you have to hike in like Augustus T. Dowd and earn your marvel by a sensationally lovely but untaxing hike. Drive to South Grove (or bicycle—good bicycling in the park!) and park. Cross pretty Beaver Creek—notice the tiny plaques nailed on the end of each bridge board, honoring a park supporter—and head off for the Big Trees.

The park offers a well-written guide for sale at the trailhead. It is an interpretive guide explaining what visitors see along the way. The last time I visited the

South Grove we double-timed out after seeing the Big Trees and hiked up the fisherman trail alongside Beaver Creek until we found a good place to splash around.

The fishing was good, too, as a strapping young lad proved by pulling two chunky trout from his creel for our inspection. He was wading around the creek barefooted and showed us his blue toes after he put away the fish. "Don't feel a thing," he cheerfully exclaimed.

Back at Oak Hollow Campground, my wife marveled at the clean, hot showers—quarter metered, but $.50 gets you a completely adequate wash-up. The campsites are nicely arranged, with enough space and brush between them so you don't feel crowded in. Between campsites 123 and 124 a trail heads down to the river. Going the other way, you come to the overlook.

Just down the road is Arnold. The supermarket is down past the golf course on the north side of the road. Before the course, on the south side of the road, is a sporting goods store where you can get fishing licenses, gear, and some friendly advice from the owner.

Don't forget to see Columbia State Historical Park. A huge hit with kids and adults, this a restored gold-rush town offers gold panning, stagecoach rides, mine tours , and cold beer at the saloon.

It is worth it to reserve if possible. I always like to camp on the periphery of the campground so the backyard of the campsite is the woods. I also like to be as far away from the campground entrance and the bathrooms as possible. At Oak Hollow sites 128, 125, 124, 123, 113, 112, 96, 95, 94, 93, 91, 90, 86, 85, and 83 are among the best.

KEY INFORMATION

Oak Hollow Campground
Calaveras Big Trees State Park
P.O. Box 120
Arnold, CA 95223

Operated by: California Department of Parks and Recreation

Information: (209) 795-2334; http://parks.ca.gov

Open: All year for limited grounds

Individual sites: 31 sites for tents only, 21 sites for small RVs up to 18 feet, 5 sites for RVs up to 30 feet

Each site has: Picnic table, fire pit, grate, camp stove

Registration: By entrance; reserve by phone, (800) 444-7275, or online, www.reserveamerica.com

Facilities: Water, flush toilets, showers, wood for sale

Parking: At individual site

Fee: $12; $8.65 nonrefundable reservation fee

Elevation: 4,800 feet

Restrictions:

Pets—On leash only

Fires—In fireplace

Vehicles—RVs up to 30 feet

Other—Reservations on holidays and summer weekends recommended

To get there: from Angels Camp on Highway 49, head 26 miles north on Highway 4 through Arnold to Calaveras Big Trees State Park. Oak Hollow Campground is a few miles from the park entrance.

PINE MARTEN CAMPGROUND

Stanislaus National Forest, Lake Alpine

CAMPGROUND RATINGS

Beauty:	★★★★★
Site privacy:	★★★★★
Site spaciousness:	★★★★★
Quiet:	★★★★
Security:	★★★★★
Cleanliness/upkeep:	★★★

When the snow melts, Pine Marten Campground is heaven. There's blue sky and blue lake with jumping fish and miles of trails to hike on. A haul to get here, but it's well worth it.

Pine Marten Campground is on pretty Lake Alpine below Ebbetts Pass. It is popular, so try to come early on busy summer weekends to get a good site near the water. If you strike out, there are several other campgrounds within rifle shot where you can pitch your tent (there is a Ranger Station just west of Lake Alpine where you can inquire). Best to come by Thursday and plan on staying a week. This is prime Sierra Nevada camping.

Ebbetts Pass, just east of Lake Alpine, was named for Major John Ebbetts, who crossed the Sierra Nevada here while looking for a route to build a railroad. He got the nominal credit, but he certainly wasn't the first man to cross here. For tens of thousands of years Native Americans climbed the Sierra Nevada looking for cool weather and food. Their trails went to food sources and summering campgrounds. So when the first gringos tried to follow their trails, they were often frustrated when they found themselves dead-ended at piñon forests and streamside flats.

Rightly, Ebbetts Pass should be named Jedediah Smith Pass because Smith was the first European to make it over the Sierras, in 1827. It was rough-going in the snow. "I started with two men, seven horses, and two mules, which I loaded with hay for horses and provisions for ourselves, and started on the 20th of May, and succeeded in crossing it in eight days,

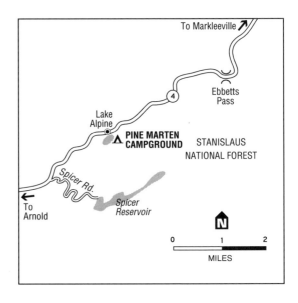

having lost only two horses and one mule. I found the snow on the top of the mountain from 4 to 8 feet deep, but it was so consolidated by the heat of the sun that my horses only sank from half a foot to one foot deep." That's from a letter to William Clark, of Lewis and Clark, then Superintendent of Indian Affairs.

It snows heavily and frequently in this area. In July 1995, the snow drifted 30 feet deep at Pine Marten Campground. Pacific storms sucked in through the Golden Gate head east to the Sierra Nevada below Ebbetts Pass. At about 7,000 feet, the clouds cool down and dump all their moisture as snow.

The last time I camped at Pine Marten Campground, in early June, I found snow drifts still there. Over the phone, the Forest Service told me the campground was open. I mentioned this to a Lake Alpine local who remarked, "Well, they don't see much driving around in their fancy pickup trucks, now do they?"

We parked our car in front of the first deep drift and carried our tent and gear into the campground, until we found a nice, level, fairly dry spot and pitched the tent. Our drinks went into a drift and I scoured dishes with snow.

Lying there in the tent at night I could feel the breeze blow off the snow drifts, chilling the air and bringing back memories of a winter camping weekend with the Boy Scouts. A blizzard blew in out of nowhere and pinned us in for a couple of days. Our Boy Scout leader was a veteran of World War II and the Battle of the Bulge, so he knew cold. When the mercury hit 20 below he made all of us put on our winter jackets and double up in the sleeping bags. The next morning we heard a tractor. Pretty soon a big green John

Deere appeared out of the driving snow, pulling a farm wagon with one anxious parent riding in it. We packed up our gear, jumped in, and that was it.

A good hike out of Pine Marten Campground is to Inspiration Point. It gets steep in places, but you can get there and back in an hour or so. Pick up the trail just past the Pine Marten Campground entrance. There's a trailhead sign for Inspiration Point/Lakeshore Trail. Follow it through the lodgepoles until you start to climb. The slopes are steep and made of weird stuff called lahar, which was left by volcanic mudflows. The views are spectacular.

Up top, we sat down on a rock and ate a pound of sweet cherries we'd bought in the farmland below and gazed at Lake Alpine basin. It looked like a perfectly natural mountain lake. Not so, Pacific Gas & Electric dammed up Silver Creek to make Lake Alpine.

The next day we went fishing in a rented boat. No luck. I got a lecture from the previously mentioned local about how to affix my worm to the hook. He also asserted that using half a nightcrawler worked better than the whole worm.

It didn't matter anyway. Lake Alpine is gorgeous. There are islands of pines and gray rock—lots of trout for other people to catch, and warm rock to lie on while looking up at the clear cerulean sky. There are hot showers at the resort as well as a great little bar/restaurant. Rent a boat and explore the shoreline. Hike up the mountains, come back, and jump into the water. It can't get any better.

To get there: from Arnold, drive 29 miles north on Highway 4, past Calaveras Big Trees State Park, to Lake Alpine (the town and lake) and the campground entrance on the right just past both of them.

KEY INFORMATION

Pine Marten Campground, Stanislaus National Forest
Forest Supervisor
19777 Greenley Road
Sonora, CA 95370

Operated by: U.S. Forest Service

Information: (209) 532-3671, (209) 795-1381; www.r5.fs.fed.us/stanislaus

Open: July through October (depending on road and weather conditions); if gate is locked, the grounds are closed; opens after last snow

Individual sites: 33 sites for tents or RVs up to 22 feet

Each site has: Picnic table, fireplace

Registration: At entrance

Facilities: Water, flush and vault toilets

Parking: At individual site

Fee: $14.50

Elevation: 7,400 feet

Restrictions:

Pets—On leash only

Fires—In fireplace

Vehicles—RVs up to 22 feet

Other—Don't leave food out

SIERRA NEVADA

SAND FLAT CAMPGROUND

Stanislaus National Forest, near Dardanelle

Set by the Clark Fork of the Stanislaus River, Sand Flat Campground is charming. For once, the best campsites are the tent-only sites. These ten sites are labeled A through J and are down by the river with lots of elbow room. There are two areas to park your car in the campground above. Except for during the spring floods, the river is languid and clean, idling around rocks and bends in the river under Sierra alders, Fremont cottonwoods, and quaking aspens. Remember to bring some old tennis shoes or water booties because good walking here is up and down Clark Fork in the water or crisscrossing from bank to bank.

Sand Flat has a laid-back feel. People come here with kids to spend a week or two in the summer. The elevation, about 6,200 feet, is easy to get used to and not too hard to take when you're hiking. At nearby Clark Fork Campground (1 mile) there are showers available for $3 a pop from 7 A.M. until 10 P.M. Kids ride their bikes on the road and run around the campground at night like wild Indians. The store at Dardanelle (population: 2), a couple miles east on CA 108, has ice, beer, sodas, hot dogs, and canned goods, so most campers arrive well supplied with basic foods.

The campground feels well run. The host comes around to collect your fee and answer any questions you might have. I liked this—it reminded me of the old days when the ranger used to come around,

CAMPGROUND RATINGS

Beauty:	★★★★★
Site privacy:	★★★★★
Site spaciousness:	★★★★★
Quiet:	★★★★
Security:	★★★★★
Cleanliness/upkeep:	★★★★

By Dardanelle (population: 2), Sand Flat Campground is in the boonies but has infinite charm and beauty. Here beats the heart of the Sierra Nevada.

welcome you, and make sure you weren't an escaped ax murderer. The water is good and comes up from the ground via a hand pump. Use a bucket to get water in because the spigot won't feed containers with little mouths. At night it was fun to walk up and down the road that goes past the campground and look at mountains against the stars and sky.

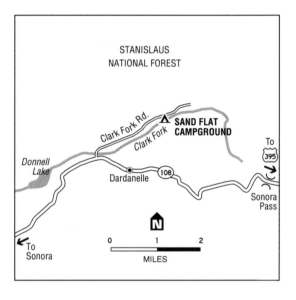

There's a good hike from Iceberg Meadow at the end of Clark Fork Road. The trailhead is on the right as you face Iceberg Peak. This is a pretty easy hike. The trail heads gently up, mostly following the Clark Fork. About 2 miles up, there are some good places in the river to swim. I quit there, went swimming, and had lunch. I met some other hikers coming down who had continued up to Boulder Creek, went left, and climbed up to Boulder Lake. They said it was a pretty lake, but little. "Not much bigger than a puddle," said a hiker from Alabama who was wearing his Donald Duck T-shirt.

Another good hike is up to Sword Lake. Plan on making a day of it as the round-trip is about 6 miles. Drive back on Clark Fork toward CA 108. About 1 mile before the intersection, take a right just before the bridge at a sign for Fence Creek Campground. Drive 6 miles to the end of the road. The County Line Trail is straight ahead. This is the best advice. Go straight ahead unless you see a trail sign advising you otherwise. Sword Lake is bright and blue and perfect for swimming. If you want to go on, there's another lake, Lost Lake, a quick stroll away. If you head around the west side of Sword Lake, you'll come to Lost Lake.

Another good excursion is to drive up to Sonora Pass. This is a hair-raising drive. Shoulderless, the road switchbacks up to 9,626 feet, where the rocks meet the sky. This was not a favorite emigrant route. The Bidwell-Bartleson party came this way in 1841 and had a harrowing time of it. As Josiah Belden remembered, "The way was very rough, and one day, in winding round the side of a mountain, we lost four of our animals, who missed their footing, and rolled down the mountain. We finally reached the summit with great labor and difficulty, and after getting beyond the summit on the other side, we struck a little stream of water that seemed to run westward and by following the stream as well as we could, it would lead us down the westerly slope of the mountain." Belden went on to become the first mayor of San Jose.

Check out the volcanic peaks known as the Dardanelles. The Dardanelles? Aren't these the rock formations in Turkey by the strait between the Aegean Sea and the Sea of Marmora (the Hellespont of ancient times)? Not so, but mapmaker George H. Goddard back in 1853 thought so.

As you look down from the Sonora Pass summit, remember the bridge that Gary Cooper blew up in *For Whom the Bell Tolls.* Look familiar? That's where they filmed the movie. Feeling hungry? The famous Burger Barn is just 30 miles east at Bridgeport as the crow flies. Then drive a little farther south on U.S. 395 to visit Bodie State Historical Park and the mines that made the Sonora Pass Road possible. It took mules and a wagon three weeks to make the round-trip supply run from the town of Sonora to Bridgeport. But what a beautiful ride!

KEY INFORMATION

Sand Flat Campground, Stanislaus National Forest
Calaveras Ranger District
P.O. Box 500
Hathaway Pines, CA 95233

Operated by: U.S. Forest Service

Information: (209) 795-1381; www.r5.fs.fed.us/stanislaus

Open: May to October (depending on road and weather conditions)

Individual sites: 10 sites for tents only

Each site has: Picnic table, fireplace, stoves; no drinking water available

Registration: At entrance

Facilities: Well water, pit toilets, access for the disabled

Parking: At individual site

Fee: None

Elevation: 6,200 feet

Restrictions:

   Pets—On leash only

   Fires—In fireplace

   Vehicles—RVs up to 22 feet

   Other—Don't leave food out

To get there: from Dardanelle, drive 3 miles west on CA 108. Turn right on Clark Ford Road, and go 7 miles to the Sand Flat Campground on the right.

SIERRA NEVADA

SARDINE LAKE CAMPGROUND / SALMON CREEK CAMPGROUND

Tahoe National Forest, near Sierra City

Wonderful Salmon Creek trills past the Salmon Creek Campground, and Sardine Lake Campground is a mile away, just below the Sardine Lakes. Nestled into the still pristine Gold Lakes area, these campgrounds have it all: excellent fishing and hiking, fabulously beautiful scenery, and even a golf course. But come for the creek and the little lakes.

Scooped out of the flank of Sierra Buttes (elevation: 8,587 feet), Lower and Upper Sardine Lakes are classic glacier tarns caused by the carving and scouring action of a glacier as it passed over bedrock. The low spots filled with water and became— tarns. How beautiful! The Sardine Lakes are blue and clear and mirror the snow and rocks in the Sierra Buttes above. (Read John Muir's *The Mountains of California* for a rhapsodic description of the life of a tarn, in the chapter titled "The Glacier Lakes.")

No wonder the forty-niners fell in love with California, despite the wicked hand Lady Luck dealt them. Still, they remembered the beauty of California, and when Charles Nordoff (author of *California for Travelers and Settlers*) came through in 1872, he found that many of the forty-niners had stayed or returned Gold Countryto live out their days.

Every site at Sardine Lake Campground has a full view of the Sierra Buttes. The last time I was there, they were brushing out the campground, so we moved half a mile

CAMPGROUND RATINGS

Beauty:	★★★★★
Site privacy:	★★★★
Site spaciousness:	★★★★★
Quiet:	★★★★
Security:	★★★
Cleanliness/upkeep:	★★★

These twin campgrounds, Sardine Lake and Salmon Creek, show the best the Sierra Nevada has to offer in an area not yet overwhelmed by visitors. Come quick.

away to the Salmon Creek Campground, where our site backed up to the creek. Many of the sites there offer views of the mountains, but the rushing waters of Salmon Creek are equally scenic. The only fly in the Salmon Creek Campground ointment is the road on the hill above the campground. From time to time, the muffler on a lumber truck overwhelms the splash of the creek, but this is a national forest, land of many uses.

A few hundred yards up toward Sardine Lake is Sand

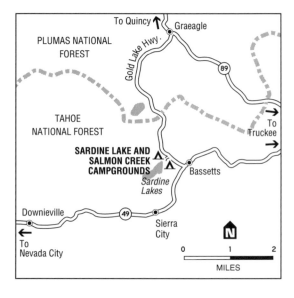

Pond, which offers good swimming. It is round, a couple hundred yards across, and shallow enough so the light-sand bottom picks up the sun. In early June, Sand Pond is warm enough to sit in the water in an aluminum chair with a book. Formed by a mining operation of the nearby All American Gold Mine, Sand Pond is prime for aquatic kids.

Early in the morning, Sardine Lake is besieged with fishermen who troll slowly across the water (5 mph speed limit) before disappointment or triumph brings them in for lunch. Some of them stay in the neat cabins at the foot of the lake. I'm told the food in the lodge there is spectacular. I eyeballed the menu in the window and it looked decidedly haute cuisine. We met an older gent fishing nearby who told us he rents a cabin every summer on Sardine Lake.

He told us about the hummingbirds, too. It seems there are seven species of hummingbirds in Northern California, and six of them breed around Sardine Lake. I've actually seen and identified five of them. The rufous, the calliope, Anna's, the broad-tailed, and the black-chinned. They come iridescent green, blue, and red, beating their wings about 75 times per second, with their hearts pumping 500 times a minute. They are so quick and small you need binoculars to really take a measure of them. The prettiest is the smallest, the calliope with exotic reddish throat whiskers. This little bird strengthens its nest with spider silk.

Later in the summer, good places to spot hummers are up by Donner Memorial State Park or down on the west shore of Lake Tahoe near D. L. Bliss State Park. Remember, if you don't see flowers, you won't see hummingbirds.

There's a fun little hike near the Sardine Lake Campground. Go toward Sand Pond, and you'll see the beginning of the Sand Pond Interpretive Trail. Immediately, the trail takes you through a "ghost" forest caused by some beavers who dammed up Salmon Creek and flooded the forest, killing all the lodgepole pines.

For lunch do as we did, drive north on Gold Lake Road to the turnoff to Frazier Falls. The parking lot and trailhead is a mile or so down the dirt road. Take a stroll into the falls lookout, then a backtrack to the granite rocks at the head of the falls. Picnic looking out over the mountains and valley.

For a great sunset, head for Upper Sardine Lake. There's an old logging trail that goes up the north side of Lower Sardine Lake. Hike up here about a mile, and—voilà!—there's another heartbreakingly beautiful but smaller tarn where you can watch the sun sink in the west and praise the angel that brought you to the Sardine Lakes.

> **T**o get there: from Sierra City, go north on Highway 49 about 5 miles to the junction with Gold Lake Highway. Go 2 miles north to the entrance to Sardine Lake Campground on your left. For Salmon Creek Campground, stay on Gold Lake Highway a few hundred yards more to the entrance on your left.

KEY INFORMATION

Sardine Lake or Salmon Creek Campground, Tahoe National Forest
Forest Supervisor
P.O. Box 6003,
631 Coyote Street
Nevada City, CA 95959-6003
www.rs.fs.fed.us/tahoe

Operated by: U.S. Forest Service

Information: (530) 265-4531, (530) 288-3231; www.r5.fs.fed.us/tahoe

Open: June through October (depending on road and weather conditions)

Individual sites: Sardine Lake—29 sites (15 for trailers); Salmon Creek—31 sites (7 for trailers)

Each site has: Picnic table, fireplace

Registration: At entrance

Facilities: Water, vault toilets

Parking: At individual site

Fee: $12; $5 for extra vehicle

Elevation: 5,800 feet

Restrictions:

Pets—On leash only

Fires—In fireplace

Vehicles—RVs and small trailers allowed (no hookups)

Other—Don't leave food out

SIERRA NEVADA

SILVER CREEK CAMPGROUND

Toiyabe National Forest, east of Ebbetts Pass

Camping at Silver Creek Campground is like sleeping on the shoulder of a huge beast—the Sierra Nevada—which is a huge hunk of granite thrust from the earth. Tilted so the western slope is gradual, the east side rises almost straight up. Silver Creek Campground hangs on like a flea just below the 8,730-foot Ebbetts Pass. The campground is on a piece of land like the prow of a ship, with the Ebbetts Pass Road running down the center. The north side of the campground has Silver Creek on its flank, the south side Noble Creek. The campsites are well engineered and clean—scoured by the winter and the dry desert air from below.

Native Americans came up both sides of the Sierra Nevada in the summer to escape the heat. It was easy to walk up over the pass and visit with folks from the other side. Yokuts from the west traded deer, antelope, and elk skins; baskets; acorns; and seashells for piñon nuts, red paint, strong bows backed with sinew, pumice stones, and obsidian from the Paiutes on the east.

The first white man to attempt the Sierra Nevada crossing was Jedediah Strong Smith. He came through California from the south with a band of trappers in 1826. Looking for beaver in the streams running down out of the Sierra Nevada, Smith noted "a great many Indians, mostly naked and destitute of arms, with the

CAMPGROUND RATINGS

Beauty:	★★★★★
Site privacy:	★★
Site spaciousness:	★★★★★
Quiet:	★★
Security:	★★★★★
Cleanliness/upkeep:	★★★★

Silver Creek Campground makes you feel the massive Sierra Nevada. Good hiking and fishing, too.

exception of bows and arrows, and what is very singular among Indians, they cut their hair to the length of three inches. They proved to be friendly. Their manner of living is on fish, roots, acorns and grass."

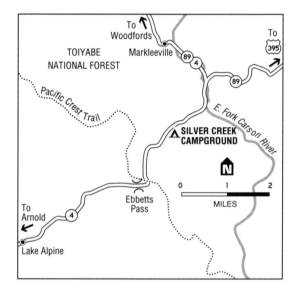

Eager to get back to rendezvous at the Great Salt Lake, Smith and his men failed in two attempts to cross going up the Kings River and the American River. Finally, Smith led his men up a Native American path along the Stanislaus River and over the mountains, near what now is called Ebbetts Pass. They arrived at the Great Salt Lake with only one horse and a mule. They ate the rest of the livestock along the way.

At Silver Creek Campground watch the stars move across the night sky, and imagine you're on the deck of a huge ship—this hunk of granite that slides across the earth over the hot magma below. From time to time, a lone car's lights come down the pass. You feel the power of the mountains and sense the fear of the drivers, the inadequacy of their mechanical conveyances, and the coming snow, which will stop them all dead in their tracks. Old Jedediah Smith must have felt that way—awed, far from home, and scared to death.

A good day hike from camp is up Noble Creek to Noble Lake. Noble Creek is the stream by the south campground area. Follow the stream up the mountain until you meet the Pacific Crest Trail. Go left on the trail and zigzag up through the granite and sage. When you reach the top, Noble Lake is off to the right. What a beautiful spot! To my companions' horror, I actually jumped in and took a dip in the gelid water.

A less rigorous way to reach Noble Lake (although still a day hike) is to drive up to the top of Ebbetts Pass. Park at the summit or a couple hundred yards down the pass toward Silver Creek Campground where there is a turnoff. The Pacific Crest Trail is marked. Head out under the pines. When I was last there in July 1996, there was a bumper crop of lupine. Hike up through the mule ear, then down toward Noble Canyon and Noble Creek, through the hemlocks and pines to where the Noble Creek Trail from the campground hits the Pacific Crest Trail. From there, you just climb up to the top of Noble Canyon and see Noble Lake on the right.

A shorter hike is into Upper Kinney Lake. This is about 4 miles round-trip and takes off a couple hundred yards east of Ebbetts Pass. Find the Pacific Crest Trail sign on the north side of the road, which is where you'll start hiking. You'll see Lower Kinney Lake on the right, then find a split in the trail signed for Upper Kinney Lake. Go left. Find Upper Kinney Lake. This is a great place to spend the day. The hiking is easy (round-trip should take about 2 hours), and I saw an angler actually pull a nice-sized trout from the lake.

Many folks who stay at Silver Creek Campground are there for the fishing on Silver Creek and down on the Carson. Markleeville is convenient for supplies, and it also has a cute little museum. There's Grover Hot Springs State Park just west of Markleeville, with a swimming pool and hot springs, which are open for a small fee. You can also go the other way west of Ebbetts Pass and visit Upper and Lower Highland Lakes, or head farther west to Lake Alpine. (Upper and Lower Highland Lakes and Lake Alpine appear in the entry for Upper and Lower Highland Lakes Campground.)

KEY INFORMATION

Silver Creek Campground, Toiyabe National Forest
Forest Supervisor
1200 Franklin Way
Sparks, NV 89431

Operated by: U.S. Forest Service

Information: (775) 882-2766; www.r5.fs.fed.us/htnf

Open: June through October (depending on road and weather conditions)

Individual sites: 22 sites for tents and RVs

Each site has: Picnic table, fire ring

Registration: At entrance; reserve by phone, (877) 444-6777, or online, www.reserveUSA.com

Facilities: Water, vault toilets

Parking: At individual site

Fee: $9; $8.65 nonrefundable reservation fee

Elevation: 6,800 feet

Restrictions:
   Pets—On leash only
   Fires—In fire ring
   Vehicles—RVs up to 22 feet
   Other—Don't leave food out

To get there: from Markleeville, go 16 miles west on CA 4 to the campground. From Arnold, drive 46 miles east on CA 4 (over Ebbetts Pass) to the campground.

SILVER LAKE EAST CAMPGROUND

Silver Lake, Eldorado National Forest, near Kit Carson

Silver Lake is a great place to bring a family. With resorts and another big campground nearby, there are always enough kids running around to entertain your own. The lake is a short walk away, where the kids congregate on the shore, and back at the campground the big boulders under the red firs draw youths like bees to honey. While they are off playing their own private games, you can sit around and take it easy. Prime camping.

And this area is beautiful! "Nothing in nature I am sure can present scenery more wild, more rugged, more bold, more romantic, and picturesquely beautiful than this mountain scenery." That's how one early pioneer described it. Of course, CA 88 is the Carson Pass Road, and it was Kit Carson who led Captain John Fremont, with his bodyguard of Delaware Native Americans, to the crest in 1844.

But it was the Mormon Brigade who engineered the wagon road. In fact, three of their number died in a Native American attack at Tragedy Springs, just southwest of Silver Lake. They were found naked in a shallow grave. The Native Americans probably killed them for their clothes. Many were inordinately fascinated with European clothing at the time—so fascinated, in fact, that they would sometimes dig up the corpses of expired forty-niners to get their clothes, and often they would contract whatever disease it was that had

CAMPGROUND RATINGS

Beauty:	★★★★★
Site privacy:	★★★
Site spaciousness:	★★★
Quiet:	★★★
Security:	★★★
Cleanliness/upkeep:	★★★★

Silver Lake East Campground is a good place to bring kids who, with any luck, will entertain each other while you relax.

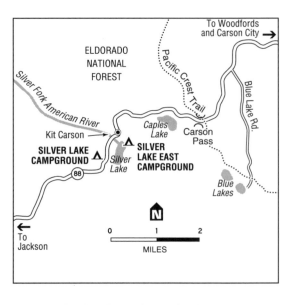

killed the unfortunate pil-
grim in the first place.

If you come over the
mountaintop from the west
and look down at beautiful
Silver Lake and the granite
cliffs around it, you'll see
that Silver Lake, like Caples
Lake above it, is in a basin
called a cirque. Cirques are
formed when glaciers eat
into the rock at its upper
end. The ice slides down
and takes the quarried rock
with it, making room for
more ice. Soon enough it
digs out a basin. Usually,
these basins or cirques
appear in a series called paternosters—like Caples Lake and Silver Lake—so
named because the lakes are in a string like beads in a rosary.

Fishing Silver Lake is good fun, as it is not as heavily fished as nearby Lower
Bear River Reservoir or Caples Lake. A cartop canoe or an inflatable is fine,
since the lake is narrow and protected. There are also boats for rent at Silver
Lake. Look for brook, brown, and rainbow trout. Most fishermen I saw headed
for the northwest corner of the lake near the boat ramp, or they fished near
Treasure Island, where the American River comes into the lake. Ask at the bait
shop for what the fish were hitting the day before and where, and follow suit.

While dad's fishing, mom and the kids can go hiking. A great hike is up to
Shealor Lake. It's about 3 miles round-trip and just perfect for a day hike,
incorporating lunch and a dip. Find the trailhead by driving 1.2 miles west of
the Kit Carson Lodge (great cabins at the lodge if you're tired of the tent)
turnoff from CA 88. There's a sign for Shealor Lake and a parking lot. Head
up through the trees and climb the granite slope to the top of the ridge. The
gnarly-looking trees out in the wind are juniper and stunted lodgepole pines.

Circle down through the rocks to the lake and jump in. Where the rock cliffs fall away to ledges, the water warms up in the sun. The temperature is almost tenable for the non–polar bear. What a beautiful little lake!

Another good hike for lunch and a dip is up to Granite Lake. Drive past Kit Carson Lodge on the east side of the lake to the north entrance of the Campfire Girls Camp. See the sign for Granite Lake and hike up through the Jeffrey pines and lodgepoles. Good hiking shoes are a must since the granite ledges are treacherous. Cross a bridge and keep going straight at a trail intersection. It is only 1 mile from the trailhead to Granite Lake, but bear in mind that 1 mile uphill on a trail is like 4 miles on a flat sidewalk. When you see Granite Lake, you'll want to jump in and chill off.

Phone ahead before coming. The Carson Pass area is famous for snow. Indeed, on the first foray by the Mormon battalion, they ran into snow so deep a donkey fell into a drift and buried himself up to his ears. Fortunately, the men were able to grab the afflicted donkey by his ears and drag him to safety. The Mormons held off their trip until July, when more of the snow had melted. So be sure to phone ahead so you don't arrive and find the place snowed in.

If you reserve, mention that you are tent camping because there are tent-only sites. These all seemed to be farther off the highway than the RV-capacity sites. Also, don't count on buying much more than ice and beer locally—bring everything else in from Jackson down the hill.

To get there: from Jackson, drive 52 miles east on CA 88 to the campground entrance on the right, past the Silver Lake dam.

KEY INFORMATION

Silver Lake East Campground, Eldorado National Forest
Forest Supervisor
Amador Ranger District
26820 Silver Drive
Pioneer, CA 95666

Operated by: U.S. Forest Service

Information: (530) 644-6048, (209) 295-4251; www.hwy88camping.com

Open: June through November (depending on road and weather conditions)

Individual sites: 28 sites for tents, 34 sites for tents or RVs, 15 reservable sites

Each site has: Picnic table, fireplace

Registration: At entrance; reserve by phone, (877) 444-6777, or online, www.reserveUSA.com

Facilities: Water, pit toilets

Parking: At individual site

Fee: $13; $8.65 nonrefundable reservation fee

Elevation: 7,200 feet

Restrictions:

Pets—On leash only

Fires—In fireplace

Vehicles—No bicycles on trails

Other—Don't leave food out; must purchse desolate wilderness permit 7 days prior to stay; 14-day stay limit

SPICER RESERVOIR CAMPGROUND

Stanislaus National Forest, off Ebbetts Pass Road

Spicer Reservoir Campground is like an ugly dog you've got to love because he hunts so well. The whole place looks like it was made by a drunk on a bulldozer run amok. Trees are all down, their big bare trunks all over the place like mastodon bones. You get there and suffer from visual shock. Then, if you don't run in horror, but set up a camp instead, suddenly the place starts to grow on you. You realize how friendly it all is and what incredible things there are to do.

Come in off CA 4 from Angel's Camp. It's not a bad trip from Los Angeles, and it's easy to access from San Francisco and Sacramento. Stop in Angel's Camp if you have time—eat at the Gold Country Kitchen on Main, which sets out a good breakfast and lunch. Not far from here, a local, Bennager Rasberry, found gold when he was cleaning his muzzle-loader and accidentally discharged it into a manzanita bush. The blast revealed gold hanging on the bush roots. The boom was on.

Continue on CA 4 toward Spicer, up past Arnold (the last good supply point for groceries, fast food, and supplies), to unfortunate Tamarack, where Forest Service Road 7N01 (signed Spicer Reservoir Road) takes off south. Poor little Tamarack holds the world record for snowfall in one winter—73.5 feet. Imagine. That's 25 yards of snow—12 men standing one on top of another. That's why God invented skis and

CAMPGROUND RATINGS

Beauty:	★★
Site privacy:	★★★
Site spaciousness:	★★★
Quiet:	★★★
Security:	★★★★
Cleanliness/upkeep:	★★★★

Ugly, but fun—Spicer Reservoir Campground is a great place for canoeing, hiking, and exploring.

---

snowshoes, and why rabbits have such big feet.

It's about 8 miles to the campground. You pass Stanislaus River Campground about 4 miles in on the right. Check it out. The sites are along the river, in among the trees. If the river is not up at spring flood, this is a great place to camp. Kids love it. It is great wading (bring water booties), and there are pools where the water backs up, warms up, and makes a wonderful place to dip in on a hot summer's day.

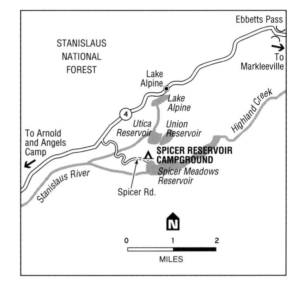

Drive another 4 miles to Spicer Reservoir Campground. Take a look at the water. A huge part of it—the long finger in the canyon to the east—is for nonpowerboats only. This makes it perfect for canoes or kayaks (even small sailboats). It gets a little breezy up there to use the small inflatables, unless you don't mind being stranded over on one side or another of the reservoir. Rent canoes or kayaks for the weekend in the flatland and cartop them up to Spicer. Once you paddle the canyon that pushes its way into the Carson Iceberg Wilderness, you'll want to own your own craft. Many rental places let you take the weekend rental off the purchase price of something new.

Right from the campground you can hike the 10 miles down to Sand Flat (see Sand Flat Campground entry). Only a walking fool could turn around and go back up in one day, so arrange a car shuttle (although it's a long way around via Sonora or the passes) or take a sleeping bag down with you and spend the night at Sand Flat Campground. There are good sites down by the stream. It's best to hike halfway to Corral Meadow and come back to camp. The trail is not too difficult, and the scenery is incredible—an ocean of granite with bursts of wildflowers in the meadows.

Another great hike is up to Rock Lake. Drive back to Forest Service Road 7N01. Go right 4 miles to the trailhead marked Elephant Rock Lake. The trail splits immediately. Go right. The second time the trail splits you can go left to see Elephant Rock Lake—pretty, with lily pads and flowers on the shore. Go right around the shore to get back on the Rock Lake Trail. Go straight through pines and fir and hit another split in the trail. Go straight and climb up into Carson Iceberg Wilderness and the Sea of Granite. You should reach Rock Lake in an easy hour's hike (about 2 miles).

I never get beyond Rock Lake. This is such a great place to have lunch and swim. There are little rock islands all over the place on which you can beach yourself and loll in the sun like a walrus. Bring a pair of water booties, as the lake is shallow and it's fun to splash around.

Or, I was told, one can also make a loop back to the trailhead, which is a longer hike by a mile or two. Go past Rock Lake to a junction for Highland Lakes. Go right here to another junction, where you go right for Summit Lake. Follow the signs for Summit Lake until you cross Forest Service Road 7N01 that you took in to the trailhead. Go right and walk up the road to your car.

I found Spicer Reservoir Campground a good base for further adventuring. In addition to canoeing and hiking the trail, I liked hiking around the reservoir. There's a fisherman's trail part of the way, and then you have to scramble, but the granite makes for good traction on your hands and seat of your pants. Spicer also makes a good first camp for dispersed camping up along the roads to Utica and Union Reservoirs. You can get drinking water and use the telephone down at Spicer.

KEY INFORMATION

Spicer Reservoir Campground, Stanislaus National Forest
Calaveras Ranger District
P.O. Box 500
Hathaway Pines, CA 95233

Operated by: U.S. Forest Service

Information: (209) 795-1381; www.r5.fs.fed.us/stanislaus

Open: Mid-June through October (depending on road and weather conditions)

Individual sites: 60 sites for tents or RVs

Each site has: Picnic table, fireplace

Registration: At entrance

Facilities: Water, vault toilets

Parking: At individual site

Fee: $12 (no reservations)

Elevation: 6,300 feet

Restrictions:

Pets—On leash only

Fires—In fireplace

Vehicles—RVs and trailers allowed

Other—Don't leave food out

To get there: from Angels Camp, go 32 miles east on Ebbetts Pass Road (CA 4) to Spicer Reservoir Road (Forest Service Road 7N01), and go right. The campground is 8 miles south.

TRUMBULL LAKE CAMPGROUND

Toiyabe National Forest, near Bridgeport

S et down by three tiny jade lakes on the backside of Yosemite, Trumbull Lake Campground is getting popular. It is primitive (no showers), but most of the campsites are reservable. People come back every year. The store in the nearby Virginia Lakes Resort sells beer, ice, and basic supplies. The access road in is paved and straight. The fishing is good, the hiking superb. Views of the snowy mountains rising around the three lakes take your breath away. Everybody you meet is complicit, because they are in on the secret that this is the most beautiful spot on earth.

The campground is on a slope above Trumbull Lake. The tiny lake by the Virginia Lakes Resort is over the hill, and the third lake is just up the gravel road a few hundred yards. The campground is like a scruffy dog. You don't like the way it looks, but after a while you learn to love it. The sites are not well engineered. Many are set too close together or too close to the pit toilets—especially the sites down by the lake. You get the feeling the campground evolved haphazardly, but, hey, here you are, on the far side of nowhere, pretty close to God.

The drive in is spectacular. Come from Los Angeles, and drive up U.S. 395 through the Mojave Desert, the Owens Valley, and up past Mammoth and Mono Lakes. This is the most spectacularly diverse terrain in California, with tons of

CAMPGROUND RATINGS

Beauty:	★★★★★
Site privacy:	★★
Site spaciousness:	★★★
Quiet:	★★★★★
Security:	★★★★★
Cleanliness/upkeep:	★★

Don't mind the campground itself. You come for the lakes, the mountains, and the big sky.

stuff to do on the way. You can also head up from Los Angeles along the west side of the Sierras, and come across on CA 120 through Yosemite National Parks.

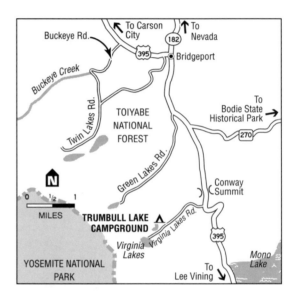

From San Francisco, take CA 108 over the Sonora Pass, where the granite meets the clouds at 9,626 feet. This was the old Sonora and Mono Toll Road, and the men who cut the road had sangfroid. Make sure your flivver is in good nick, and hang on to the steering-wheel. It is wild and beautiful—where *For Whom the Bell Tolls* was filmed with Gary Cooper.

I bought salmon eggs and power bait in Lee Vining and caught a decent-sized trout on hooks trimmed of the barb so that I could release (since Tuesday is always spaghetti night). My older sister came along—her first time in the Sierra Nevada for 40 years—and we sat out in the meadow among the lupine and forget-me-nots with a star map and looked up at the sky.

The next day we hiked up to the trailhead by Blue Lake (there's a trail from the campground from site 5 that connects with the trail past the trailhead) and hiked a mile up to Frog Lakes. This is up around 10,000 feet, so expect to suck some air. Take your time and rest often—the older you get the longer it takes to get acclimated to the rarer air. Then we plugged on to Summit Lake on the Sierra Ridge between Camiaca Peak and Excelsior Mountain to the south. We stopped for sandwiches and soda chilled in the cold lake water and watched storm clouds close in around Excelsior Mountain (elevation: 12,446 feet) before we scooted back down to the campground just ahead of a completely unseasonable (early July) thundershower, replete with ear-cracking thunder, hearty gusts of wind, and frightening white streaks of lightning.

Cringing in our tent under the pines, I regaled my sister with tales of old John Muir, who loved storms and climbed to the top of the highest pine and tied himself in while the elements raged around him and shouted Walt Whitmanesque exaltations to the primal gods. And John didn't come back to his tent and a towel; he camped in an old overcoat with his sundries in the pockets. He survived one bone-numbing night by crawling into a hot mud spring—alternating cooking one side of himself and freezing the other.

The next morning the sky was as clear blue as the sea, and the chirping sparrows flitted from bush to flower in the meadow. We borrowed an inflatable boat from a camping neighbor and floated around the lake, trailing a little bait and staring up at the mountains above the basin.

I spoke to the campground host (from L & L Inc.) who told me they had plans to make more of the campsites reservable. I checked out all the sites. Sites 10 through 13 are lakeside with a great view, but see-heavy traffic and are near a pit toilet. I preferred the campsites off the lake, around the fringes of the camp. Site 14 was my favorite. After that came sites 4, 5, 7, 8 (not site 6), and 35 through 37. Still, the campsite itself doesn't really matter. Shortly after arriving at Trumbull Lake Campground, as soon as you take a good look around at the mountains and water, you'll know you're home.

To get there: from Bridgeport, go about 14 miles south on U.S. 395 to the Conway Summit. Go right (west) on Virginia Lakes Road and drive 6 miles to the campground on the right. From Lee Vining, drive about 12 miles north on U.S. 395 to the Conway Summit and go left (west) on Virginia Lakes Road. Drive 6 miles to the campground on the right.

KEY INFORMATION

Trumbull Lake Campground, Humboldt-Toiyabe National Forest

Bridgeport Ranger District
HCR 1 Box 1000
Bridgeport, CA 93517

Operated by: U.S. Forest Service

Information: (760) 932-7070,

Open: June 9 through September (depending on road and weather conditions; opened July 1 in 1996)

Individual sites: 45 sites for tents or RVs

Each site has: Picnic table, fire ring

Registration: At entrance; reserve by phone, (877) 444-6777, or online, www.reserveUSA.com

Facilities: Water, vault toilets

Parking: At individual site

Fee: $9; $8.65 nonrefundable reservation fee

Elevation: 9,500 feet

Restrictions:

Pets—On leash only

Fires—In fire ring

Vehicles—RVs up to 35 feet

Other—Don't leave food out, no swimming in lake

SIERRA NEVADA

UPPER AND LOWER HIGHLAND LAKES CAMPGROUND

Stanislaus National Forest, near Ebbetts Pass

This campground is my favorite campground in the Sierra Nevada. At 8,600 feet, the campsites are by the pretty little Highland Lakes, in a valley full of bright wildflowers. If you can get in on the road to Highland Lakes, it means the snowdrifts have melted. If the snowdrifts have melted, you know the wildflowers are out—this is a short season. To the north, even in late August, Folger Peak has snow fields. Hiram Peak to the south is as big and brown as a warm bear. There are hikes going everywhere. This is off the beaten track. You don't just happen to show up there. Plan to stay for a while.

The Highland Lakes are up on the west side of Ebbetts Pass. This area is notorious for snow. Some years the pass is snowed in until August. In July 1995 the snow at Lake Alpine a thousand feet farther down was drifted 30 feet deep. Pacific storms get sucked in through the Golden Gate and head east to the Sierra Nevada below Ebbetts Pass. At about 7,000 feet the clouds cool down and dump all their moisture as snow. Lots of snow.

Well, it's not much easier going now until the drifts melt, and the county plows the road, and the days get warm, and flowers bloom in the meadows, and planted fish run in the streams. The dirt road in off CA 4 is rough-going but easily managed by even the wimpiest of sedans. Just go slowly and mind the bumps. It takes off to

CAMPGROUND RATINGS

Beauty: ★★★★★
Site privacy: ★★★★★
Site spaciousness: ★★★★★
Quiet: ★★★★★
Security: ★★★★★
Cleanliness/upkeep: ★★★★★

*Come prepared to stay.
My favorite Sierra Nevada
campground.*

the southeast just 1 mile below Ebbetts Pass (14.5 miles above Lake Alpine). The road (Forest Service Road 8N01) goes down a steep hill, then runs along pretty Highland Creek filled with wonderful places for dispersed camping, if you thought ahead for the requisite permit (free at any Ranger Station) and have a bucket and shovel for fire suppression. Some of the area is designated Rehabilitation Project, meaning you can walk in and enjoy, carry a tent in, and camp, but you

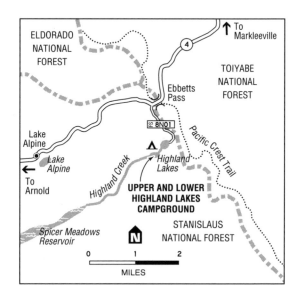

can't drive your vehicle in. Of course, where it is not posted you can drive in on existing access roads and camp by your car.

Pass fields of purple lupine and crazy shooting stars and a wonderful old-style line ranch, and after a steep climb, there are the two Highland Lakes and Lower Highland Lake Campground on the right under lightning-blasted pines. The sites are not well designed, but they are pretty and clean. There's one outhouse near the middle of camp and a pump for water across from site 10. Remember to bring a bucket for hauling water from the pump to your campsite.

To reach the Upper Highland Lakes part of the campground, take the dirt road that goes west between the two lakes. It has a confusing sign that appears to advise four-wheel drive only. Ignore this. The road to the camp area (only a few hundred yards long) is just like the road you drove in on. Any sedan can make it easily. These sites are just above the lakes in a stand of pines. Right away, you'll see the pump and outhouse. The campsites are back in under the pines and a short walk from the Upper Highland Lake. If you want privacy, camp up here. If you have kids who want to run around, or if you like the western sun to warm your bones, camp in the Lower Highland Lakes area below, where it is sunnier and flatter.

Bring supplies. The nearest store is at Lake Alpine, or east to Markleeville. Bring an extra cooler filled with ice and duct-tape the top. Leave coolers in the shade. Put a wet cloth over the coolers and let evaporation cool the outsides. Think about buying one of those coolers you can fold up afterward as an extra. Bring water booties for the lake. Think about bringing a little inflatable Sevylor-style boat (at chain stores everywhere for $50 or less) to float around in with a book and fishing gear (brook trout). Buy a Lake Alpine Carson–Iceberg Wilderness map for $1.95 at the Lake Alpine store so you can navigate the trails around the lakes. (Or buy the more ambitious Forest Service map at any nearby Ranger Station.) Remember sunscreen, as the air is thin and the sun strong. Remember to bring Chap Stick and skin lotion, as it is dry. Bring cotton balls (good for stanching the flow) if the kids tend to have nose bleeds. Borrow from the other campers if you forget anything—most campers are friendly and want to help by lending things they prudently remembered to bring along themselves.

Camping at Upper and Lower Highland Lakes Campground requires a little extra forethought and travel time. But it's worth it. Remember, phone ahead to get road conditions, to find out whether the campground is open, and to see if drinking water is available. If there is no drinking water, boil lake water (five minutes at a roiling boil), or buy a water filter from a camping store.

KEY INFORMATION

Upper and Lower Highland Lakes Campground, Stanislaus National Forest
Forest Supervisor
19777 Greenley Road
Sonora, CA 95370

Operated by: U.S. Forest Service

Information: (209) 532-3671, (209) 795-1381; www.r5.fs.fed.us/stanislaus

Open: June through September (depending on road and weather conditions—be sure to phone ahead)

Individual sites: 36 sites for tents

Each site has: Picnic table, fireplace

Registration: At entrance

Facilities: Well water, pit toilets

Parking: At individual site

Fee: $8

Elevation: 8,600 feet

Restrictions:

Pets—On leash only

Fires—In fireplace

Vehicles—Large RVs or trailers not recommended

Other—Don't leave food out

To get there: from Arnold, go 29 miles east on CA 4 to Lake Alpine. Continue 15 miles past the Lake Alpine store to Forest Service Road 8N01 (signed to Highland Lakes) on the right. At this point, you will be 1 mile west of Ebbetts Pass. Drive 7.5 miles in on a graded dirt road.

UPPER JAMISON CAMPGROUND

Plumas-Eureka State Park, near Graeagle

D rive into Mohawk Valley on your way to Upper Jamison Campground, and all of a sudden you are in the land of lush green golf courses and condos. Graeagle, just 5 miles from the park, is a retirement mecca. Graeagle has elegant restaurants, a good grocery store, a deli with smoked meats, and a pond with a great swimming beach right in the center of town.

The nearby Feather River Inn used to be the most fashionable resort in Northern California. Passengers arrived on the train, and porters pushed their steamer trunks over in wheelbarrows. Now the flannels and black cocktail dresses with pearls have given way to ski parkas or golf shirts, depending on the season, but the area still has a sense of style and gentility.

Drive into Plumas-Eureka State Park. The rangers are polite and friendly. Everything is tasteful and under control. The museum is thoughtfully done. The handout pamphlets (many and detailed) are grammatically correct. Drive another mile or so to the Upper Jamison Campground at the end of the road. By pretty Little Jamison Creek, the campsites are well separated and nicely screened from one another by trees. The bathrooms are rough but clean. The whole camping experience is enjoyable, though a little removed. Maybe it's the areas rich history that gives you the Westminster Abbey feeling of strolling among the bones of kings and commoners

CAMPGROUND RATINGS

Beauty:	★★★★
Site privacy:	★★★★
Site spaciousness:	★★★★
Quiet:	★★★
Security:	★★★★★
Cleanliness/upkeep:	★★★★

Camping at Upper Jamison Campground is an experience in style and gentility. Only the bears are rowdy.

whose hopes, dreams, and sins are now all dust.

Indeed, except for nearby Jamison City's (now Johnsville) brief raffish period replete with fisticuffs and fancy women, the area has always been respectable. Johnsville was a company mining town with solid citizens brought in from Wales, Austria, and elsewhere to work the mines and live in harmony in the company town (now all buried in the local Johnsville cemetery—worth a visit).

Only the bears are rude.

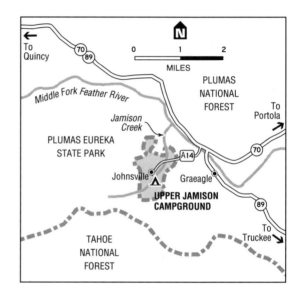

Folks are implored to cooperate with the rangers to keep those naughty ursines in line. Don't leave food around while you are not in the area. Keep a clean camp. Put your food and coolers in your trunk when you do leave. If you have a hatchback, disguise the coolers with a blanket or haphazardly placed clothes. Bears are smart, strong, and very hungry. They have been known to tear open an automobile like a sardine can just to get a tube of sunscreen.

Naturally, we were there for two days and didn't see a bear. We did see the work of beavers up at Madora Lake, as well as Canada geese, coots, and a glimpse of what might have been a fox around dusk on our walk. Directions to Madora Lake are quite clear in the Plumas-Eureka State Park handout. In fact, you passed the turnoff to the lake on your way in from Graeagle.

Walking in and around Madora Lake takes about an hour. On the far side of the lake is a picnic table, perfect for a sandwich or a sundowner while you look for beaver. This industrious rodent practically fueled the western exploration. During the late 1700s and early 1800s, explorers headed west as they decimated the eastern beaver population. They cured the pelts and sent them to factories where the hair was made into felt, which was then made into the beaver top hats. These hats held their shape and repelled water and were the rage for a while.

When beavers became trapped out and the beaver hats passé, the next rage was human scalps, which inspired a market at least as spirited as the beaver-pelt market. Adult, child, Mexican, Anglo, or Native—the scalps, when properly cured, commanded top dollar in Europe as curios and in the East for their medicinal properties.

Now the beavers have aggressively bounced back and can be seen around Plumas-Eureka State Park (another sure beaver sighting hotspot is Lake Earl Wildlife Area just north of Crescent City). Beavers like streams around aspen, birch, alder, and willows. They get out most in the summer after the birth of their kits and work mainly in the early morning and evening.

Another great hike is up the Grass Lake Trail, where you will find even more beaver signs. Grass Lake is pretty and surrounded by Jeffrey pine and red fir. Work your way around to the west side of the lake to get the best view of the incredible mountains on the other side.

Don't miss camping at Plumas-Eureka. But remember, Upper Jamison Campground is first come, first served, so plan accordingly. Pay your fee in the office in the museum if it is before closing time; otherwise, just drive down to the campground, occupy a site, and pay the fee the next morning when the charming ranger comes around in her truck.

To get there: from Graeagle, take Highway 89 north to Highway 70. Take Highway 70 west to County Road A14. Five miles west on CR A14 is Plumas-Eureka State Park. Go left past Park Headquarters to the campground at the end of the road.

KEY INFORMATION

Upper Jamison Campground Plumas-Eureka State Park 310 Johnsville Road Blairsden, CA 96103

Operated by: California Department of Parks and Recreation

Information: (530) 836-2380; http://parks.ca.gov

Open: Late May through September (until it snows)

Individual sites: 67 sites for tents, trailers, or RVs

Each site has: Picnic table, fireplace

Registration: At office in museum by entrance; reserve by phone, (800) 444-7275, or online, www.reserveamerica.com

Facilities: Water, flush toilets, hot showers, wood for sale

Parking: At individual site

Fee: $12; $8.65 nonrefundable reservation fee

Elevation: 5,200 feet

Restrictions:

Pets—On leash only

Fires—In fireplace

Vehicles—RVs and trailers up to 30 feet

Other—No burning of dead or downed wood— purchased firewood only

SIERRA NEVADA

WOODS LAKE CAMPGROUND

Eldorado National Forest, near Woodfords

The first look at Woods Lake makes your head swim. This tiny blue gem is surrounded by mountains reaching to the sky. Waterfalls flash silver as they fall down from the melting snowfields. Boulders and islands along the water's edge glow warm and gray in the high-altitude sun. The needles are soft under the pines. A few fisherfolk float around, fly casting in their waders and inflatable devices. A family paddles by in a canoe (no motorboats allowed). Then you see the campground.

Woods Lake Campground is precious. Set up for tent campers, the first 14 or so sites have the fireplace and picnic table set well back from the parking space. You pitch your tent among the red penstamenemblazoned rocks, or down in a hollow, or up on a hillside. You have to come Sunday afternoon through Thursday to get a spot here. People come back year after year. One woman with her daughter has been coming for 20 years. Eagerly, she asked me which site I'd found. When I told her, she said, "Oh, that's where we brought her [indicating her lovely college-aged daughter] when she was first born."

Think about water. Woods Lake Campground is plumbed for water, but there has been a failure of some kind. So the only available water is a 180-foot-deep well accessed by a hand pump in front of campsite 18. It takes two to pump water. One vigorously manipulates the handle (it

CAMPGROUND RATINGS

Beauty:	★★★★★
Site privacy:	★★★★★
Site spaciousness:	★★★★★
Quiet:	★★★★
Security:	★★★★★
Cleanliness/upkeep:	★★★★★

Make an effort to camp here— prettiest lake camping in the High Sierra. Plan to stay a week.

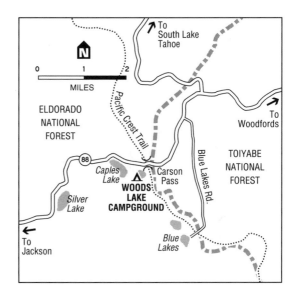

takes about 20 pumps to bring up the water) while the other person holds the water jug. It's not a bad idea to bring a bucket or a funnel since the water comes out of the pump spigot in a way that makes it difficult to direct it into a narrow-neck jug. You work for it, but the water is so sweet.

I arrived July 1996 with my East Coast older sister, and we immediately trekked around the lake in our go-aheads (flip-flops). Good thing, too, since where the waterfalls ran into the lake you had to wade knee-deep to cross. Then there was the swamp on the far side of the lake that we avoided by climbing up over the rocks and down the other side, risking life and limb to cross yet another quickly moving stream before we found the trail back to the campground.

There are two trailheads near the campground. From either, you make a big arc through Winnemucca Lake, Round Top Lake, and back down to Woods Lake. The full trip is about 5 miles. Remember to watch the weather—it can snow here just about any time. It's not a bad thing to carry in your pack along with your sweater those emergency rain parkas (buy them in a camping store) that could give you a margin of comfort if it does start storming. Access one end of the trail from the day use parking lot near Woods Lake. Cross the bridge over the stream and follow the signed trail to Winnemucca Lake. At first you walk on the shoulder of a moraine (a ridge of rubble left by a retreating glacier), then into a pine forest. Spot the *arrasta* (a Mexican mining device for breaking up ore) on the right. Then the trail breaks out into an incredible meadow filled with acres of wildflowers tumbling up toward the ridge and sky above. What an incredible sight! Only later when we chatted with a nice woman hiking with a huge slobbering hound did we learn that this wildflower spot is famous for display.

Soon enough you come to Winnemucca Lake (named for a Paiute chief from Nevada), a sharp blue shard of water set in weathered-gray granite. Two daring young hikers hastily breaststroked across to a warm boulder and flopped up on it like pink seals. Otherwise, there was just the sough of the wind across the rocks and stunted pines.

A four-by-four signpost directs you to Round Top Lake. (Read this style of signpost directionally. Standing where you can read the direction, go forward.) There's more huffing and puffing to Round Top Lake, then the trail swings down around Lost Cabin Mine (posted against trespassers) and drops you at the campground near sites 14 through 16.

Fishing at Woods Lake and Winnemucca Lake is indifferent. I saw a few folks down at Woods Lake pull in some ten-inch rainbows at the Woods Creek end of the lake. But fishing here is not about what you catch, obviously. It is a religious experience, and most people seemed to approach it that way.

The little Carson Pass Information Center a few miles east on CA 88 is worth visiting—at least to see what books and pamphlets they have about the area. Read, too, the plaque outside about old Snowshoe Thompson. This old boy was tough as nails and makes our iron men of today look like a bunch of poofters.

Remember to bring supplies. Caples Lake Resort has a tiny store that sells ice, beer, and fishing gear but not much else. The nearest real grocery store is across the pass at Woodfords. For campers who strike out at Woods Lake, I suggest going over the pass to the Blue Lakes.

KEY INFORMATION

Woods Lake Campground, Eldorado National Forest
Forest Supervisor
100 Forni Road
Placerville, CA 95667

Operated by: U.S. Forest Service

Information: (530) 644-6048, (209) 295-4251; www.r5.fs.fed.us/eldorado; www.hwy88camping.com

Open: May through September (depending on road and weather conditions)

Individual sites: 25 sites for tents

Each site has: Picnic table, fireplace

Registration: At entrance

Facilities: Piped well water, pit toilets

Parking: At individual site

Fee: $10, extra vehicle $5

Elevation: 6,650 feet

Restrictions:

Pets—On leash only

Fires—In fireplace

Vehicles—No RVs or trailers

Other—Don't leave food out; use bear boxes

To get there: from Jackson, drive east 70 miles on CA 88 past Caples Lake to the turnoff to Woods Lake Campground on the right. Go about 2 miles. The campground entrance is on the right before you reach Woods Lake.

WRIGHTS LAKE CAMPGROUND

Eldorado National Forest, near Riverton

Reserve your site months ahead. Bring the kids, because Wrights Lake Campground is perfect for all ages of kids. It's small and cozy. The lake is clean and warm, ideal for swimming off the rocks and shore or from canoes and small inflatables on the water. This is a made-to-order movie set for a coming-of-age film. The campground is small and intimate. For once the tent-only sites get the best real estate—down by the lake—while the RVers are off on the other side of the dam. The sites are private, with boulders and coppices of pines blocking one from another. The plateau area that Wrights Lake occupies is sylvan and warm with crisscrossing streams—more meadow than the harsher Oceans of Granite farther south toward Yosemite.

This place is popular. Folks from Sacramento and San Francisco plan a year ahead to spend their vacations here. Everybody has a smile on their face. All you can hear is the sound of birds singing and the kids splashing into the water and laughing. Even the campground's namesake was a happy guy. Friends on an expedition in 1881 wrote about James William Albert Wright that "Captain Wright was the only fleshy member of our party. His ribs were so encased in such thick layers of fatty tissue that, knowing his inability to freeze, we elected that he should sleep on the windward side of the camp."

CAMPGROUND RATINGS

Beauty: ★★★★★
Site privacy: ★★★
Site spaciousness: ★★★
Quiet: ★★★
Security: ★★★
Cleanliness/upkeep: ★★★

Reserve ahead. This is the best place to bring kids. It is stunningly beautiful, too.

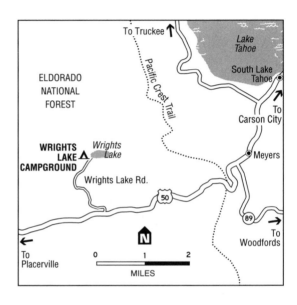

You have to bring some flotation device. Motorboats are not allowed, so midnight paddles are a widespread Wrights Lake practice. New, light, rooftop canoes or kayaks are best adapted to the lake, but any inflatable will do. Go for one of the Sevylor-style jobs for about $50 in Big 5 or Sportmart. Buy an electric pump to plug into your car's cigarette lighter, and a repair kit. These inflatables are fun on high mountain lakes. They get you out of the freezing water, off the shore, and into the sun.

Wrights Lake is accessed from U.S. 50. Once called the Placerville Road, U.S. 50 was built as a toll road by Colonel John Calhoun (Cock-Eye) Johnson. He made a ton of money on wagons heading for Virginia City (well worth a visit—go on a weekday). Cock-Eye's toll road was rumored to be "five feet deep by a hundred and thirty miles long and composed mostly of mountains, snow and mud." Now cars and buses (gambler's specials) fly up and down this road. It is kind of unnerving, and you'll need to watch carefully for the Wrights Lake Road, which comes abruptly on a curve, so be mindful of the frantic traffic.

Bring lots of ice and supplies. The nearest reliable gasoline, ice, and grocery towns are in Meyer to the east over Echo Summit, or Riverton to the west. Bring an extra cooler packed with ice and duct-taped shut. Put a wet blanket on it and cool it by evaporation. Put drinks in a little six-pack cooler so folks won't be opening and closing the food cooler all day long. Make a menu and stick to it—it's amazing how little food you need if it is planned. Don't count on "living off the lake," although people do catch rainbow and brown trout—

it is stocked and some of the brown trout that survive through the winter get to be pretty big boys.

Hiking around Wrights Lake is fun. Many of the other day hikes require permits you can conveniently get at the Wrights Lake Campground. The last time I was up there, we hiked up to Smith Lake. The hike is a killer but has the asset of leaving from the campground. Just hike up the road on the east side of Wrights Lake to the Twin and Grouse Lake Trailhead. Cross the fence and walk up through the meadow. At the beginning of July it was packed with flowers.

After maybe half a mile the trail splits. Go right up the slope. The trail climbs. Pass a sign for the Desolation Wilderness, and go right when the trail splits. When you reach a trail signed for Twin/ Island Lake, go right again. This climb is a bear until you get to Grouse Lake. If you have any sand left in you, go left around the shore and follow the trail through the swamp up to Hemlock Lake.

Keep going to the right of Hemlock Lake, and stagger on up the mountain to Smith Lake. This lake is good dipping, and you're going to need it. You've only walked 4 miles from the campground, but 3 of them have been straight up. Imagine how you'd feel if you were carrying a 50-pound pack. No wonder John Muir went hiking in his great coat with all his provisions in his pockets.

Reserve Wrights Lake as much as a year in advance so that you'll get one of the tent-only sites on the lakeshore. . The best time for us West Coast folks to call is about 6:00 P.M. Since the center is on the East Coast, most folks back there should be getting ready for bed, so the lines won't be so busy.

KEY INFORMATION

Wrights Lake Campground, Eldorado National Forest
Forest Supervisor
100 Forni Road
Placerville, CA 95667

Operated by: U.S.Forest Service

Information: (559) 622-5061, (530) 644-6048, (530) 644-2349; www.r5.fs.fed.us/eldorado; www.hwy88camping.com

Open: July through October (depending on road and weather conditions)

Individual sites: 35 sites for tents only, 36 sites for tents or RVs

Each site has: Picnic table, fireplace

Registration: At entrance; reserve by phone, (800) 444-7275, or online, www.reserveUSA.com

Facilities: Water, pit toilets

Parking: At individual site

Fee: $13; $18 for double sites; $8.65 nonrefundable reservation fee

Elevation: 7,000 feet

Restrictions:

Pets—On leash only

Fires—In fireplace

Vehicles—RVs up to 22 feet; motorboats prohibited

Other—Don't leave food out

To **get there:** from Placerville, drive 34 miles east on U.S. 50. Turn left on Wrights Lake Road (watch the turn—it's dangerous), and go 8 miles up the narrow road to the campground.

APPENDICES

APPENDIX A
Camping Equipment Checklist

Except for the large and bulky items on this list, I keep a plastic storage container full of the essentials of car camping so that they're ready to go when I am. I make a last-minute check of the inventory, resupply anything that's low or missing, and away I go!

Cooking Utensils
Bottle opener
Bottles of salt, pepper, spices, sugar,
    cooking oil, and maple syrup in
    waterproof, spillproof containers
Can opener
Corkscrew
Cups, plastic or tin
Dish soap (biodegradable), sponge,
    and towel
Flatware
Food of your choice
Frying pan
Fuel for stove
Matches in waterproof container
Plates
Pocketknife
Pot with lid
Spatula
Stove
Tin foil
Wooden spoon

First Aid Kit
Band-Aids
First aid cream
Gauze pads
Ibuprofen or aspirin
Insect repellent
Moleskin
Snakebite kit (if you're heading for
    desert conditions)
Sunscreen/Chap Stick
Tape, waterproof adhesive

Sleeping Gear
Pillow
Sleeping bag
Sleeping pad, inflatable or insulated
Tent with ground tarp and rainfly

Miscellaneous
Bath soap (biodegradable), washcloth,
    and towel
Camp chair
Candles
Cooler
Deck of cards
Fire starter
Flashlight with fresh batteries
Foul-weather clothing (useful year-
    round in the Northwest)
Paper towels
Plastic zip-top bags
Sunglasses
Toilet paper
Water bottle
Wool blanket

Optional
Barbecue grill
Binoculars
Books on bird, plant, and wildlife
    identification
Fishing rod and tackle
Hatchet
Lantern
Maps (road, topographic, trails, etc.)

APPENDIX B
Suggested Reading

Best Short Hikes in California's Northern Sierra. Whitehill, Karen and Terry. The Mountaineers, 1990.

California Camping. Stienstra, Tom. Foghorn Press, 1994.

Easy Camping in Northern California. Stienstra, Tom. Foghorn Press, 1995.

Easy Hiking in Northern California. Brown, Ann Marie. Foghorn Press, 1995.

Exploring the North Coast. Franks, Jonathan. Chronicle Books, 1996.

Gem Trails of California. Mitchel, James R. Gem Guides Book Co., 1986.

Gold! Gold! Petralia, Joseph F. Sierra Outdoor Products Co., 1992.

History of the Sierra Nevada. Farquhar, Francis P. University of California Press, 1965.

Humboldt Redwoods State Park. Rohde, Jerry and Gisela. Mile & Miles, 1992.

Mendocino Coast. Lorentzen, Bob. Bored Feet Publications, 1995.

A Natural History of California. Schoenherr, Allan A. University of California Press, 1992.

Northern California Handbook. Weir, Kim. Moon Publications, Inc., 1995.

Redwood National & State Parks Tales, Trails, & Auto Tours. Rohde, Jerry and Gisela. Mountain Home Books, 1994.

Roadside Geology of Northern California. Alt, David D. and Donald W. Hyndman. Mountain Press Publishing Co., 1975.

A Treasury of the Sierra Nevada. Reid, Robert Leonard. Wilderness Press, 1983.

Walking California's State Parks. McKinney, John. HarperCollins West, 1994.

The World Rushed In. Holliday, J.S. Simon & Schuster, 1981.

APPENDIX C
Sources of Information

B.L.M., California State Office
2800 Cottage Way, Suite W1834
Sacramento, CA 95825-1886
(916) 978-4400f
www.blm.ca.gov

California Parks and Recreation
P.O. Box 942896
Sacramento, CA 94296
(916) 653-6995
www.parks.ca.gov

Eldorado National Forest
100 Forni Road
Placerville, CA 95667
(530) 622-5061
www.r5.fs.fed.us/eldorado

Humbolt-Toiyabe National Forest
    Sierra Ecosystem
1200 Franklin Way
Sparks, NV 89431
(775) 331-6444
www.fs.fed.us/htnf

Klamath National Forest
1312 Fairlane Road
Yreka, CA 96097-9549
(530) 842-6131
www.r5.fs.fed.us/klamath

Lassen National Forest
2550 Riverside Drive
Susanville, CA 96130
(530) 257-2151
www.r5.fs.fed.us/lassen

Lassen Volcanic National Park
P.O. Box 100
Mineral California 96063
(530) 595-4444
www.nps.gov/lavo

Lava Beds National Monument
P.O. Box 867
Tulelake, California 96134
(530) 667-2282
www.nps.gov/labe

Modoc National Forest
800 West 12th Street
Alturas, California 96101
(530) 233-5811
www.r5.fs.fed.us/modoc

Pacific Gas and Electric Land Projects
2730 Gateway Oaks, Suite 220
Sacramento, CA 95833
(916) 386-5164
www.pge.com

Shasta-Trinity National Forest
2400 Washington Avenue
Redding, CA 96001
(530) 244-2978
www.r5.fs.fed.us/shastatrinity

Stanislaus National Forest
19777 Greenley Road
Sonora, CA 95370
(209) 532-3671
www.r5.fs.fed.us/stanislaus

Tahoe National Forest
631 Coyote St.
Nevada City CA 95959
(530) 265-4531
www.r5.fs.fed.us/tahoe

U.S.F.S., Pacific Southwest Region
1323 Club Drive
Vallejo, CA 94592
(707) 562.8737
www.r5.fs.fed.us

INDEX

ABOUT THE AUTHOR

Working for the Denver Museum of Natural History, Bill's mother was an avid camper, and she developed in her son a love for the outdoors. Inspired by the Native American "digs" that his mother worked on and their many camping jaunts to Maine, the Adirondacks, and numerous locations in the West, Bill continued to foster his enthusiasm for camping.

Driven by his sense of adventure, Bill did a stint in Pernambuco, Brazil, after college, working for the Peace Corps on a small rancher's cooperative. Reminiscent of 1830s New Mexico, there were no cars and no electricity, but an abundance of cattle drives and gunfights in the streets.

After shaking off the chaps and spurs, Bill donned the vestments of academia to teach at several colleges around London. In the interim, he composed several short stories and a novel. Unwilling to give up his roots, he continued to camp in England, biking down old county lanes and camping in farming fields overnight.

Now Bill lives in Santa Monica, California, where he continues to write screenplays and wonderful books about his love of camping, including *The Best in Tent Camping: Southern California*, the series counterpart to this book. And of course, he continues to travel extensively on camping and fishing expeditions around Baja California and California proper.